P9-AZW-601

BECOMING YOUR OWN BEST FRIEND

BECOMING YOUR OWN BEST FRIEND

THOMAS A. WHITEMAN, PH.D.
& RANDY PETERSON

THOMAS NELSON PUBLISHERS
Nashville • Atlanta • London • Vancouver

Published in Nashville, Tennessee, by Thomas Nelson, Inc., Publishers, and distributed in Canada by Word Communications, Ltd., Richmond, British Columbia.

ISBN 0-8407-9646-3

Printed in the United States of America.

CONTENTS

STEPS TOWARD BECOMING YOUR OWN BEST FRIEND

Step 1
Make a personal inventory of pluses and minuses.

Step 2
Begin to compliment yourself in the presence of others.

Step 3
Isolate a problem in your life and take steps to correct it.

Step 4
Identify the "villains" that have damaged your self-esteem.

Step 5
Discover a source of unconditional love through a personal relationship with God.

Step 6
Decode society's sinister messages and break free of them.

Step 7
Find something you can do well and then do it.

Step 8
Get involved in the lives of others.

Step 9
Adopt this new way of thinking about yourself as part of an ongoing lifestyle.

INTRODUCTION

Deep down in his heart no man much respects himself.

—MARK TWAIN

On a recent TV interview, Billy Graham told Barbara Walters that he felt like a failure. Viewing the condition of the world, he couldn't help but feel that his mission was far from finished.

Billy Graham regularly shows up on lists of the most respected men in America. It would be difficult to find any one person who has touched so many lives as deeply as this evangelist. But despite the praises that ring in his ears, Billy Graham has his own standards. And he feels that he has fallen short.

Maybe you have felt the way Reverend Graham has. You regularly do not measure up to your own standards.

How is your relationship with yourself? Can you give yourself realistic compliments when you've done things well? Or do you put yourself down frequently? Are you more aware of your weaknesses than of your strengths?

As a psychologist, I keep seeing problems that stem from a poor self-image. And, to be honest, this nagging foe has plagued me for many years. While researching the book *Love Gone Wrong,* I became even more convinced that we need to pay serious attention to self-esteem issues.

I was interviewing single adults who had the tendency to get into unhealthy and sometimes destructive relationships. One striking common denominator in their testimonials was a low self-image.

"I knew I couldn't attract anyone better, so I stuck with this guy."

"I probably deserved the abuse."

"I stayed in the relationship because, well, I guess I can't stand being alone."

In each case, their recovery had to start with learning how to respect and enjoy themselves. These people, and many like them, need some guidance in accepting themselves before they can safely navigate relationships.

But another book? Didn't we get enough self-help in the Seventies and Eighties? Isn't "looking out for number one" old hat by now?

The problem I see with most attempts to build self-esteem is that attention is focused *entirely* on the self. People learn to put themselves first, to buckle up their courage and go out there and be selfish! But that doesn't work either.

We need to find a *balanced* way to love ourselves. We need to deal with our personal insecurities and self-doubts in a way that upholds the value of others, too. Self-sacrifice is not a bad word *if* it is balanced by a healthy appreciation of the self. That's the rhythm of life—giving and receiving.

Let me be up-front with my readers. I am a Christian, but I don't assume that you are. I believe the Bible has valuable insights and these have formed my position on certain issues, but I will not be preaching to you.

This book will present strategies for building and maintaining a balanced self-esteem. It will discuss practical ways of confronting some of the "villains"—past or present—that keep us from accepting ourselves. It will give you specific ideas and activities that may change your way of thinking about yourself.

Any book like this requires stories of people who have "been there." I offer stories from my clients and acquaintances (and myself). To protect them, I have changed names and some details in order to make the persons' identities unrecognizable, but the essential aspects of each story are true.

As part of our research, my co-author and I took an informal survey of friends and former clients. We extend our thanks to those who replied. Their responses appear here and there throughout this book. My two closest friends, Lori (my wife) and Tom Bartlett, have provided me with a lifetime of experiences and examples of how to be my own best friend; so to them I owe much more than thanks.

Thanks also to our patient editor, Vic Oliver, who helped greatly in shaping the concept for this book, and to my colleagues at Life Counseling, who have contributed their thoughts. I also owe thanks to Bob Burns and Tom Jones, who work with me at Fresh Start, for the ideas and stories I regularly borrow and develop. My co-author and I also thank Charity Slavens, Ken Petersen, Jeff Bills, and Deb Austin for inspiration and encouragement.

I hope that your story takes a dramatic turn as you read this book and apply its ideas.

—Thomas Whiteman
and Randy Petersen

CHAPTER 1

Best Friends

No man is a failure who has friends.
—CLARENCE THE ANGEL

Every Christmas, I watch the movie *It's a Wonderful Life*. You've probably seen it yourself at least a dozen times. In the movie, Jimmy Stewart's character, George Bailey, is forever helping others. All over town, he is well-liked and well-respected. This fondness is apparent to everyone—that is, everyone but George. He feels depressed and hopeless. He's in a rut and feeling bad about himself because he hasn't been able to accomplish the things he had set out to do.

We know what it is to feel that we haven't accomplished our goals and dreams, perhaps even to feel like a failure. Yet deep inside, we long to know that we have affected those around us, or that we are respected and loved.

For George, this revelation reaches a climax with the outpouring of love and gifts from all of his friends. The movie ends with an inscription in a book George is given: "No man is a failure who has friends."

Your life, no matter how insignificant you might feel it

is, is much more important than you realize: that's what this movie is telling us. The ripple effects of our actions extend to our family, friends, neighbors, even our entire community.

For much of my life, I saw myself as a complete failure. I tried to live up to other people's standards, and I could not do it. I desperately wanted to be better, smarter, funnier. Here and there, people tried to build me up, but it didn't work. I had no hook on which to hang their encouragement.

If only a friend could crawl inside my skin and be there with me—then I might be able to hear. It's great for all those people to show up and tell George Bailey how terrific a guy he is, but even that won't work unless there's someone *on the inside*. George needs *George* to affirm him, or at least to accept the affirmations of others. And I, in my attempt to earn the favor of others, came to a dead end. I got some positive feedback, but it didn't count. I wanted more. I needed more. I had a Teflon self-image—nothing stuck. It was like trying to store a computer document in a directory that does not exist. You have to create the directory first. It was like trying to deposit money in an account that hasn't been opened. There's nowhere to put it.

I needed to be my own friend. I needed to muster the courage to accept myself, with all my strengths and weaknesses, to give *myself* the affirmation I needed.

Becoming your own best friend does not mean shutting out the rest of the world, or the rest of your friends. It does mean establishing that core self, that germ of self-acceptance that can begin to grow within you. Once you get a friend "on the inside"—yourself—you can replay *It's a Wonderful Life* whenever you need to. You can call up all the affirmations you need from that computer directory marked "Self-Esteem."

It was only when I began to treat myself as my own best friend that I began to be comfortable in relationships with others. My friendships were deepened and energized by my self-acceptance. Certainly, there have been times when life has been especially *un*wonderful, but friends help friends get through such times. And if you are your own friend, it will be much, much easier.

No man is a failure who has friends; and no man* feels *like a failure if he learns to become his own best friend.

Finding the Balance

As I have said, becoming your own best friend does not mean becoming self-centered, self-absorbed, or unaware of the needs of others. No, just as a friendship needs balance and boundaries, so our self-image needs to be balanced between self and sacrifice, giving and receiving. As you become your own best friend, you will be a better friend to others. Your relationships will be balanced and healthy.

I grew up believing that it was a sin to love myself. Any hint of pride was dangerous. I learned to be very aware of my shortcomings and to downplay whatever strengths I had. If you had told me to be my own best friend, I would have turned you off or put you down. I had a very hard time understanding how I could ever like certain things about myself, or be proud of any of my accomplishments. Life is lived for others, I would say. If you love yourself, you must be shortchanging others, or cheating God.

I was wrong.

In chapter 7, I will discuss some of the religious implications of being your own best friend. For now, it will suffice to say that it's not an "either/or" proposition; it's a "both/and." I can love God *and* love the way God made me. I can love others *and* love myself. In fact, I *must* love myself, to some extent, if I am truly to love at all. How can you "love the LORD . . . with all your heart . . . soul, and . . . mind" (Matt. 22:37 NKJV) if you reject the value of your heart, soul, and mind? How can you "love your neighbor as yourself" (Matt. 22:39 NKJV) if you hate yourself?

Best Friends

What does a best friend do? How do we define this role? If we are to confer best-friend status upon ourselves, what's the job description?

It would be hard for me to measure the value of my relationship with my best friend. He provides companionship, fun, and zest to my life. But more important, I gain from him a reliable and constant source of affirmation, support, and accountability. I know he will give me honest feedback about my ideas and dreams. He will encourage me when I'm low and bring me back down to earth when I'm going to conquer the world. I know and trust his criticism because he has earned my respect, and I know he will confront me with love and concern.

Do you have a best friend? If so, think about your relationship with him or her. If not, think about what kind of relationship you'd like to have with such a person.

What does your best friend provide in your life that's so valuable? In our own informal survey we asked, "What qualities do you look for in a best friend?" and got the following responses.

We Can Tell Them Anything and They Will Not Judge or Condemn Us

While I might appear to be quite nice to those who know me only superficially, I am capable of some rather devious thoughts. One way I define a best friend is as someone I can tell my worst thoughts and know I will not be judged. In fact, he won't even think less of me. Instead, he'll listen to me, empathize with my feelings, and then encourage me toward a more positive viewpoint. That is extremely valuable, and rare.

They Provide a Constant Source of Honest, Valuable Feedback

What makes best friends so unique is that they know us so well. When they give us feedback, it's much more meaningful than the words we get from more casual friends. I recently had an acquaintance get mad at me and make some rather critical comments about me. It bothered me for several hours, until I vented this experience to my wife. When she assured me that the comments were inaccurate, I immediately felt better. Why? First, I knew she would be honest with me. I could be sure that she would tell me if the criticism was valid. Most important, I knew that she knew me better than anyone else. She had much more evidence for her point of view than that acquaintance had for his.

They Support and Encourage Us

Most of us enjoy being with our friends because they provide a haven in an otherwise hostile world. When we feel beaten up by our bosses, or rejected by our families, or even misunderstood by our spouses, we know that our best friends are always there for us, ready to support and encourage. Not that they will excuse our bad behaviors—they will correct us when we need it; but they will do so gently and in an encouraging way.

They Hold Us Accountable

A good friend not only supports and encourages us, but also lets us know when we are out of line or headed in the wrong direction. I am able to confide some of my weaknesses to a few of my closest friends. They hold me accountable because they would be the first to see me straying. They do it in a way that assures me that they have my best interests at heart.

They Add Fun and Laughter to Our Lives

Perhaps what I love most about my best friend is that we can just get away together and have fun. For me this is usually a fishing trip, camping, or just a lunch together. He always gives me a good excuse to get away and do something just for the fun of it. Without a best friend to do these things with, I doubt that I would do them at all.

What is a best friend?

- ***A best friend will not condemn you.***
- ***A best friend will offer honest feedback.***

- ***A best friend will support you.***
- ***A best friend will hold you accountable.***
- ***A best friend will laugh with you.***

What happens if we take these principles of friendship and apply them to ourselves? How can we be our own best friends?

We Shouldn't Condemn or Judge Ourselves Too Harshly

Just as we are able to hear the worst about a friend and still accept him, we must be able to do the same for ourselves. Yet many people judge themselves by a much stricter standard than they would apply to anyone else. They seem unable to forgive themselves for mistakes or wrongdoing. This not only contributes to a poor self-image, but if it goes on extensively, it can create an identity saturated with guilt and shame.

We Should Always Be Honest and Balanced in What We Tell Ourselves—And We Should Trust Our Own Honest Feedback

What makes a friend's feedback so valuable is that it is honest and balanced—and knowledgeable. We tend to trust the judgment of our friends because (1) they care for us, and (2) they know us. We know they'll tell us what we need to hear; and because they're so close to us, they *know* what we need to hear. Can we treat ourselves in the same way?

Who knows us better than we know ourselves? Then

why do we let ourselves be floored by the critical comments of those who hardly know us at all? If we are truly honest with ourselves, we will recognize our own value, we will be neither too hard nor too soft in our self-appraisal.

Imagine a play that gets a bad review in the local paper. As the actors gather in the dressing room, one says, "I don't know how I can go onstage tonight after that review. He said I was 'laughably inept.'"

An older, wiser actor says, "Do you think you are laughably inept?"

"No."

"How do you think you're doing?"

"Well, I thought I was doing pretty well. I really thought this was the best work I've ever done."

"And how long have you been acting?" the older one asks.

"About ten years."

"And how long have you been working on this play?"

"Six weeks, three nights a week."

"So," says the experienced actor, "you've spent sixty, seventy hours on this play, and you've acted in—what?—twenty, thirty shows. This person spent two hours with the play and formed a quick impression of it. Whose opinion are you going to trust?"

We often put ourselves in the place of that younger actor. We are jolted out of our self-confidence by some "review" that criticizes us. The critic may have no idea of who we are or what we're doing, but the negative words throw us. We need to trust our own fair judgment in such cases. (But it must be *fair* judgment, not overly judgmental, as we said in the previous point.)

We Need to Support and Encourage Ourselves

I've often told people to go ahead and compliment themselves whenever they can—because if they don't, who will? Not too many of us ever get positive comments from people unless we have very positive relationships. And for most of us, our natural tendency is to put ourselves down. To become our own best friend, we need to learn to encourage and build ourselves up regularly.

In our survey, we asked people how many times in an average month they said something positive about themselves in front of someone else. Of the twenty-five who responded, about five indicated that this happened frequently—twelve to fifteen times or more per month. Another handful indicated that it hardly ever happened. And the strong majority said it happened two to four times in a month. This is clearly an unscientific survey, *not* specifically sent to people with self-esteem problems, but I think it shows us some interesting things. *Some* people have no problem talking positively about themselves, *others* have a great problem with it. Most of us are in the middle. But note where this middle ground is—two to four times a month! That's once a week or less that we feel free to say something good about ourselves in the presence of someone else! *Maybe* we find it easier to encourage ourselves in the privacy of our own minds, but I'm not even sure of that. Most of us feel awkward about praising ourselves in public; we don't want to be braggarts. But many of us translate that into a reluctance to *think* good things about ourselves. If we dare to be satisfied with a job well done, we condemn ourselves for being too proud. We need to be more courageous in this area, encouraging ourselves when we need it—just as our best friend would.

We Also Must Learn to Challenge Our Own Thinking and Behaviors

Lest we become too easy on ourselves and excuse all of our bad thoughts and habits, we must balance ourselves out by setting reasonable goals and challenges. Just as we might tactfully and lovingly confront a best friend about a dangerous activity, so we must take a critical look at ourselves from time to time. Good self-esteem does not mean blind acceptance of anything we might do. It means caring enough about ourselves to do what's best. We need to know our weakness and work toward self-improvement.

I was recently at a dinner party with several other couples. At one point the conversation grew sarcastic, and I joined in by saying something rather caustic to one of the other guests. It drew a good laugh, but I remember thinking that it wasn't very nice of me.

As I lay in bed that night, I rehashed in my mind the comment I had made and how I might have gotten a laugh at the expense of this other person. My discomfort led me to apply a major premise of this book. I asked myself, "Now if I was talking to my best friend, what would I tell him to do about this situation?" I concluded that the only thing to do was to stop beating myself up and to call the woman the next morning to offer an apology.

Our friendship was deepened with this other couple, and I learned a valuable lesson.

The key words here are "tactfully," "lovingly," "reasonable goals." A best friend does not tear you down. A best friend does not berate you without offering support. A best friend is interested in your development, your growth. So when a critical word is spoken, there is always a hopeful word for the future. "You will do better, I'm sure." "There are great possibilities for you." "Stop this and start *this;* it's the better way."

Lenny Dykstra, the high-energy lead-off hitter for the Philadelphia Phillies, has always intrigued me. The other night, I watched him at bat as the umpire called strike one on a borderline pitch. Dykstra stepped away from the plate, spat tobacco juice, and launched into a vicious tirade. Fortunately, TV does not give us the sounds of such on-the-field chatter, but it was obvious that Dykstra was swearing angrily. As far as my lipreading skills could pick up, he was saying, "You nincompoop! [Well, that wasn't exactly the word he used, but I'll be discreet.] You're terrible!" I was afraid he might get thrown out of the game. But the announcers, who know him well, said, "He's not talking to the ump. No, he's not arguing the call. He knows it was a strike. He's mad at himself for not swinging at that pitch."

All of that venom for one strike! Dykstra had already scored three runs in the game, his team was winning the game and was in first place in the league, and he was tearing into himself over one pitch. Apparently he expected himself to get a hit every time up, to swing at every good pitch that crossed the plate. He set impossibly high standards for himself and scolded himself for not achieving them.

I don't intend to psychoanalyze this ballplayer, but I've seen many people like him in their everyday lives. They expect perfection and rip themselves apart when they don't measure up. There is a better way. We must find a way to say, kindly and more gently, "Yes, I should have swung at that pitch, but there will be another. I'll do better then."

We Need to Learn How to Enjoy Ourselves and Laugh at Ourselves

In our survey, we asked, "Could you consider yourself your own best friend? Why or why not?" One person responded, "More now than a year ago. Now I enjoy time alone. I can make myself laugh. I can find many ways to have fun." In those few short sentences, we have a picture of recovery. When a person laughs easily, he or she can usually take stressful and self-defeating situations in stride. Laughing at yourself shows you understand your own weaknesses and can accept them. Critical comments or awkward situations can be absorbed gracefully.

THE BRICK AND THE SPONGE

A brick is hard, unyielding. It will resist attacks from the outside, but it might crack under pressure. So will we if we try to present a hard exterior that has no flaws. The sponge is aware of its holes. The holes make the sponge what it is. The holes make it useful. In the same way, the healthy person accepts his or her shortcomings, and even enjoys them to some extent. They are just part of who we are as we grow toward wholeness.

As we become our own best friends,
- ***we do not condemn ourselves.***
- ***we give ourselves honest, balanced feedback.***

- ***we encourage ourselves.***
- ***we challenge ourselves when we need it.***
- ***we learn to enjoy ourselves.***

Applying the Analogy

Let's examine how this analogy of the best friend helps us in real-life situations.

Carrie has been coming to me for counseling for over a year. She has been to at least two other counselors before me, always over the same issue. Carrie believes that she is stupid. According to her, she always says stupid things, and other people think she's a "ditz." Carrie is sure everyone is laughing at her behind her back. This has affected all of her relationships and has hurt her especially in the work environment. She tends to keep to herself and rarely engages in conversation. Even though she is bright and has done well in school, she is chronically underemployed because of her belief that she will fail. In a sense, Carrie is her own worst enemy, holding herself back in relationships, as well as professionally.

Carrie's beliefs about herself seem to stem from her critical parents, especially her father. She could never measure up to his standards, and he belittled her for this. She feels that she was lucky to get through college, and that she certainly didn't measure up academically to any of her peers. (After the graduation ceremony, her father said he couldn't believe they actually gave her the degree.) Her difficulty in finding employment after graduation only confirmed that she really wasn't qualified to do anything important. When she finally got a clerical job in an office, she had trouble picking up some of the skills, and the other people in the office may not have been very helpful. They kept telling her, "You're a college graduate, you should be able to figure it out." She assumed that they, too, were laughing at her.

Now, at age 28, Carrie is debilitated by her belief that she does not measure up to others. She rarely takes risks, rarely dates, and has only a few friends. Her friends think that she has a lot to offer and cannot understand why she holds herself back.

Carrie's counseling has allowed her to explore the reasons for her poor self-concept. She knows all about the guilt and shame she got from her parents, especially Dad. But the most nagging problem now is the messages about herself that continue to invade her mind:

"Keep your mouth shut, they'll probably laugh at whatever you say."

"These people don't want to hear your opinion."

"Everyone knows what to do in this situation. You must be stupid, and everyone will know it as soon as you ask that silly question."

The negative messages go on and on.

In my counseling with Carrie, I tried to get her to change those negative messages into statements that were more accurate. We worked on the problem for months. I found that Carrie could come up with more accurate self-statements when she really put her mind to it . . . while she was in my office. But as soon as she left, when she was on her own, she went right back to the old put-downs.

One week, I offered her the best-friend analogy because I could see she needed some way of conceptualizing what I was trying to say to her. "Carrie," I said, "let's imagine your best friend had the same self-image that you do. She put herself down regularly and thought that she was stupid. What would you say to your best friend?"

Carrie was able to respond immediately. She said, "I would confront her with the facts. You've got a college degree. You did well in school. Your friends, at least those who know you well, respect you. . . ." She listed several more supportive facts. Carrie was picking up the idea very quickly.

"Now," I continued, "let's take a look at a specific incident. You feel like your co-workers are making fun of you. What would you say to your best friend about that?"

Once again Carrie responded easily. "I would ask her, 'Well, how many of *them* have a college degree? Perhaps they treat you that way because they are jealous. Besides, if that's the way they want to treat you, that's their problem. You just need to do your job, and do all you can to improve yourself and get out of that office!' "

I congratulated Carrie on her good advice to her friend and encouraged her to use the same tactic each time she found herself thinking badly about herself. To this day, Carrie uses the same technique to talk herself out of her irrational thinking. She hasn't eradicated all of the negative messages—they're deeply ingrained in her mind—but she is getting better.

Recently I spoke at a church in another state. In my talk I referred to a good friend from that church who was at the meeting. I spoke highly of Bob, saying what a great guy he was, and how important he was in my ministry. I sensed a rustle of uneasiness in the audience, but I wasn't sure what it was—until later. After the talk, my friend came up to greet me. I looked at him and knew instantly what was wrong. His name wasn't Bob; it was Frank.

How embarrassed I was! I apologized profusely to him. I *knew* his name, he really was a good friend, but my mind sometimes takes a vacation without telling me. Frank took it all in good humor. He understood; no problem.

But on the drive home, I kept berating myself about it. How could I have been so stupid? It must mean that I really don't care about people as I should. Or maybe I'm just not a good speaker. Maybe I can't think and speak at the same time. I'm hopeless. Here I embarrassed myself and offended a friend. I felt awful about it.

Then I decided to take some of my own medicine. What would my best friend tell me?

"Relax, Tom. What's the problem here? You offended your friend, yes, but you apologized and he accepted. He understood completely. It's not a problem for him. Case closed.

"Ah, but you still embarrassed yourself, didn't you, Tom? You made a mistake in front of a group of people. Yikes! So now they know you're not perfect. My guess is that they knew that before you started speaking. Perfection is not a requirement for this job.

"Let it rest, Tom. It happened, and there's nothing you can do about it. But there are no major scars. You didn't do any damage—except you reminded yourself that you're only human. Let it rest."

My "best friend" in my head talked me back to self-acceptance.

CHAPTER 2

The Balancing Act

It's hard to be humble when you're so great!
—MUHAMMAD ALI

I'm usually a marshmallow. I want people to like me, so I often give in to them, even when it may not be the best course of action. That's why it was so shocking recently when my wife accused me of acting in a callous and insensitive way toward someone who had been seeking my help. Someone had called me at home on a holiday to get counseling for some crisis situation. Only I felt that the crisis could wait until normal business hours, and I said so. While my wife appreciated the priority I placed on spending holiday time with my family, she felt that I had spoken too harshly to the caller.

My wife was right. As I reviewed the situation, I realized I *had* been uncharacteristically harsh and even arrogant toward this particular person. And yet it was another step in the development of my self-image. Let me explain.

For more than a decade I have been working on my self-image, with special attention to this business of being a people-pleaser. Underlying much of what I do is the assumption that I am not as good as other people, and thus I need to win their favor by impressing them, humoring them, or being so gracious and giving that they would be attracted to me as a "nice guy." Yes, at times this has been my goal in life: to be hailed by everyone I know as a "nice guy." Yet this way of life made me frantic: I constantly wondered what people were thinking of me and how I was coming across.

A pattern developed. I would sacrifice for others, often neglecting my own needs. After being licensed as a psychologist, I sought to build my practice. In accordance with my personality, I built my business by seeing anyone, anytime, for whatever they could pay. I would volunteer to speak anywhere, on almost any topic, and rely on the kindness of my hosts to at least cover my expenses.

As you can well imagine, it didn't take long for me to become very busy. I was working all kinds of hours, but mostly early mornings and then in the evening, since that was when people preferred their appointments (so that they didn't miss work). Then I was speaking to groups or in seminars most weekends and finding that I was barely making enough to cover my expenses. Nevertheless, I kept working harder until I was so busy that I was ready to bring on another counselor as part of a newly formed counseling center. Since I really wanted this to be a ministry to the community, I set the fees according to what people thought they could afford. I relied on people's own judgment.

I was working every night until eight or nine, and then returning phone calls until the wee hours. I prided myself on the fact that I returned every call on the same day I received it because I thought this was a responsible way to do business. While this is true, it would be more honest to say that I did it because I was worried about what people would think of me if I didn't get right back to them.

My personal life suffered. My wife felt my distance, and with a new baby in the house, I could see things had to change. Yet I wasn't bringing in enough money to cut back. What was I going to do? I remember thinking, "Work just a little harder, for a little longer." I added a third and fourth counselor to the practice, but found that my headaches increased respectively.

I was beginning to feel better about myself because of my success in building a practice, but was negating everything I gained by having a family life that was less than satisfactory. My wife felt (with good reason) that everyone else was more important than she and our new baby were. I was feeling more and more trapped, and my self-concept suffered greatly

This crisis forced me to rethink my goals and priorities in life. Most of all, however, it caused me to examine my own self-image. Why was I working so hard for so little? Why was I agreeing to travel and not get paid for my time? And why didn't I let people call me back if they needed to talk to me rather than try them numerous times before I gave up? As a psychologist, I realized that the *real* question was "Why don't I have any boundaries?"

We are out of balance if we are sacrificing for others and hurting ourselves in the process.

My sense of self was out of balance. I was sacrificing for others, but not loving or protecting myself. I knew that I was motivated by the dictates of others, and worried about what they thought even after I had gone the extra mile and then some.

The first thing I did was to sit down with my wife and ask for her patience and indulgence for a little longer. I knew I couldn't change everything overnight, but knew that I needed to start right away. I promised her that within a year things would be better, and I would be more balanced.

I started by setting my fees at an hourly rate. I stopped taking any speaking engagements unless they paid for my time and travel. I limited my hours, especially at night, and I stopped making any calls outside of the office unless it was an emergency. In essence, I set up my boundaries.

Most people would see this change as an issue of time and business management. For me, it was far more than that; it was mostly a self-esteem issue. I had felt guilty charging for my time because I didn't feel I was worth it. And if I didn't charge for my speaking, people wouldn't expect very much. Besides that, I put almost no value on time reserved for myself. When I began to treasure my time more, everything had to change.

What was the result? A few people were put off by my new policies, but by far, more people were helped. They valued my time more and therefore took the counseling more seriously. They came to see me when I was available and made sacrifices to be there. I had fewer no-shows and far less in unpaid bills.

People took my speaking engagements more seriously, paid the fee, and drew larger groups. The bottom line is that the seminars grew, the practice grew, and when people really needed to talk with me, we always found a way to connect during business hours. Most important, I have more time with my family (I now have three children), I have more time for myself, and I enjoy my work more. I still worry sometimes about what people think of me, but I don't worry for very long. I'm still concerned when I don't get back to people right away, but I do the best I can in an eight-hour day. I still take speaking engagements that I should turn down, but at least I now get paid for them. I'll probably always strive to be known as a nice guy, but at least now that desire is balanced by self-esteem.

When we find a healthy balance, everyone benefits: ourselves, our family, our friends, and our co-workers.

Going Too Far

Yet now, from time to time, I go too far in the other direction. I guard my boundaries so zealously that I become too hard on people. This was the case with my holiday caller. When I begin to think I'm pretty important, or when I get stressed out over my schedule, I can begin to put people off. I can get pretty selfish.

I remember the first time I appeared on a national television broadcast. I was feeling nervous and inadequate about the appearance until I got there. They put me up in a ritzy hotel, sent a chauffeured limo to pick me up, and treated me like royalty while I was in the studio. The interview went well, and I got a lot of affirmation from a lot of people. It's a good thing it only lasted one day—any more of that and I'm not sure my head would have fit through my front door.

In my story, we see the two extremes. On the one hand, self-sacrifice is a noble thing—until it becomes self-destruction. On the other hand, it is good and necessary to protect one's personal boundaries—until this becomes selfishness.

But what does that mean for those saints who have poured their lives into service for others, the Mother Teresas and the David Livingstones of the world? Is their self-sacrifice an unhealthy thing? No, probably not. I would say that these people find a certain wholeness in ministry. It might *seem* that they are losing themselves in ministry, but they are actually finding themselves there. Even they, I believe, have to set some boundaries so that they can continue their mission. If self-sacrifice leads to self-destruction, soon there is no more "self" to give.

Then again, is it possible for people to think too much of themselves? Well, yes. If a person starts concentrating on his or her own needs and ignoring the needs of others, that person is out of balance. We humans are valuable creations, and we can enjoy our identity and celebrate our relationship with our Creator. But we are also members of the human race, created to be in community with others, caring for them even as we care for ourselves.

There are two extremes in our self-image. One is the self-sacrifice that leads to self-destruction. The other is the self-esteem that leads to selfishness. We need to learn to balance these two sides of self-love.

In their book *The Two Sides of Love,* Gary Smalley and John Trent describe this same concept, applied to the way we love others. They speak of "the hard side and soft side of love." "It's essential," they say, "that we learn to balance love's hard and soft sides every day if we want to communicate to others the deepest most meaningful kind of love." We must also learn to balance this love in our own lives.

Smalley and Trent use the illustration of the rose. It is a thing of absolute beauty, but God has seen fit to protect it by giving it thorns as well. The beauty draws us to it, perhaps to pick it, but the thorns are there to protect it. In the same way, our soft, giving side will tend to draw people to us, but we need protection, too. Just like the rose, we also need the hard side of love—the side of our self-image that protects, corrects, and sets clear boundaries when necessary.

Test Yourself

What about you? Do you tend toward self or sacrifice (see fig. 2.1)? The hard side or the soft side of love? Remember, the goal is to exhibit a healthy balance. Maybe you don't know for sure, or perhaps (as in my case) it is something that has evolved, and changes according to your levels of stress.

Sacrifice

I described my own sacrificial side, which resulted in a lack of boundaries and some general people-pleasing. But for you, perhaps it takes a different form. Here are several other examples of a self-image that leans too far toward the sacrificial.

Rescuing. This is the tendency to get into relationships in order to reform or change the other person. People with

Finding the Balance

Where on the continuum do you fall?

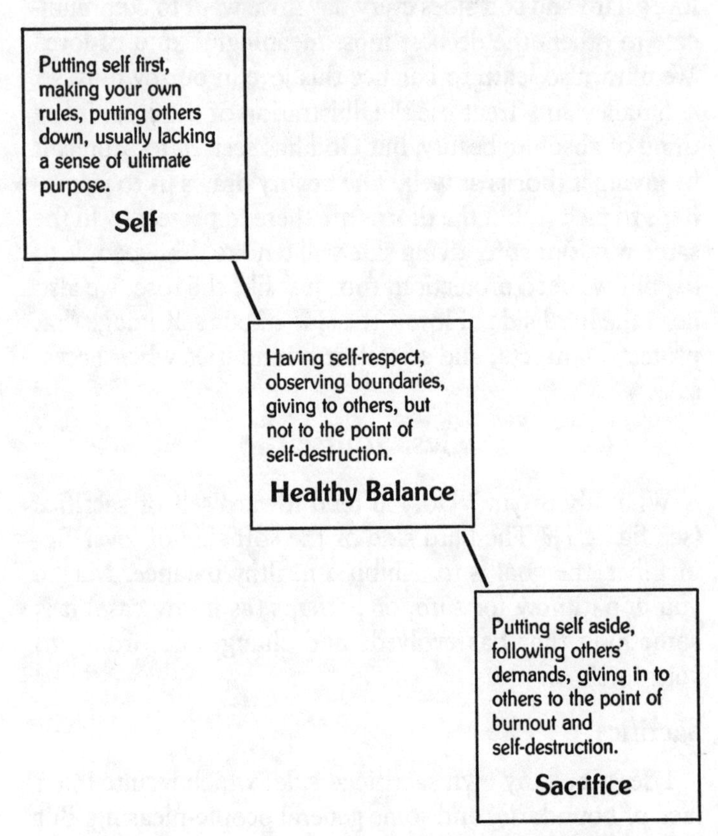

Figure 2.1. The continuum of self-image.

this tendency feel good about themselves when they are bailing someone else out of trouble or nursing them back to health.

Enabling. This tendency to cover for another person in a way that enables them to continue an inappropriate behavior is most commonly found in those who enable abuse, addictions, or manipulation of others.

Codependency. This current buzzword refers to a tendency to care more for others than for yourself in a way that is considered unhealthy. The simplest description I've heard is this: "It's okay to be responsible *to* people, but the codependent feels responsible *for* other people." The self-image of the codependent is constantly at risk because taking responsibility for others is a losing proposition.

Perfectionism. This is the most extreme example of self-questioning. Perfectionists agonize over every decision and detail, hoping for perfection, which of course they never achieve. Their lives are spent trying to measure up and therefore they end up by feeling that they are inadequate.

Self

On the other hand, there is the selfish side of self-love. In my case this was displayed through indifference, insensitivity, and a little arrogance. However, here are some of the signs of this imbalance.

Self-Centeredness. Obviously, selfish people focus on themselves and their own needs. Everyone else's problems pale in comparison. I was self-centered as I guarded my own time and neglected the needs of the person who called me. I'm not saying I should have dropped everything to help this person—that might have been too much of a sacrifice—but a more balanced approach would have been better. In its most extreme form, self-centeredness is known as "narcissism," a preoccupation with one's own needs, desires, or appearance.

Anger. When we feel that we have been wronged, we often become angry. It is a legitimate response to injustice. But the selfish person needs little provocation. The sacrificial person tips the scales of justice, letting people get away with murder. The selfish person, however, tips the scales the other way, expecting too much and getting riled over the littlest thing.

Manipulative/Controlling Behaviors. If the world revolves around you, you can do whatever you have to in order to get people to do what you want. Selfish people are usually convinced that their way is the best way, and they do anything necessary to get others to follow. (You can begin to see how people at this end of the spectrum are dangerous to those at the other end. There are users and usees, and they tend to find each other.)

Compulsive/Impulsive Behaviors. We often see these tendencies in people who act first and then think later, after it's too late, how their actions might affect others.

Myopic Views/Blind Spots. When a person focuses on self, he or she generally misses much of what's going on. Such people become rather myopic, or short-sighted. They focus on their own needs and miss the fact that others around them are in need. This can also lead to blind spots or weaknesses that are apparent to others but of which they themselves are unaware. Even when others point out their weaknesses, they may ignore the advice because they seldom consider outside perspectives.

HOW SELFISH OR SACRIFICIAL AM I?

As you consider these lists and your own tendencies, where do you fall on the continuum between Self and Sacrifice? Perhaps this test will help you decide. This is not a definitive study, merely a simple evaluation. It will only be as helpful as you are honest.

On a scale of 1 to 10, where do you fall on the following continuum?

1. When with my friends and choosing what to do on a particular evening, I tend to

Do whatever they want — Take the lead

1 2 3 4 5 6 7 8 9 10

2. When expressing an opinion, I tend to

Doubt my own convictions — Insist that I'm right

1 2 3 4 5 6 7 8 9 10

3. When in a new social setting I will tend to

Keep to myself — Be outgoing and friendly

1 2 3 4 5 6 7 8 9 10

4. I worry about what other people think of me. — I do what I think is right and don't worry about other people's opinions.

1 2 3 4 5 6 7 8 9 10

5. I sacrifice my own good for the needs of others. — I take care of myself first and most frequently.

1 2 3 4 5 6 7 8 9 10

6. If asked to address a group on a topic I am familiar with, I would feel

Inadequate and scared — That they were lucky to have me

1 2 3 4 5 6 7 8 9 10

7. When I meet people who obviously have a lot of problems

I feel a sense of responsibility to rescue them — I head for the quickest exit

1 2 3 4 5 6 7 8 9 10

8. When a friend is criticizing me, I

Feel bad, rejected — Ignore it

1 2 3 4 5 6 7 8 9 10

9. When others express their opinions, I

Assume they know more than I do — Tend to think they don't know what they're talking about

1 2 3 4 5 6 7 8 9 10

10. When a friend stops over unexpectedly, I tend to

Worry about not having something to serve them — Be bothered by the interruption

1 2 3 4 5 6 7 8 9 10

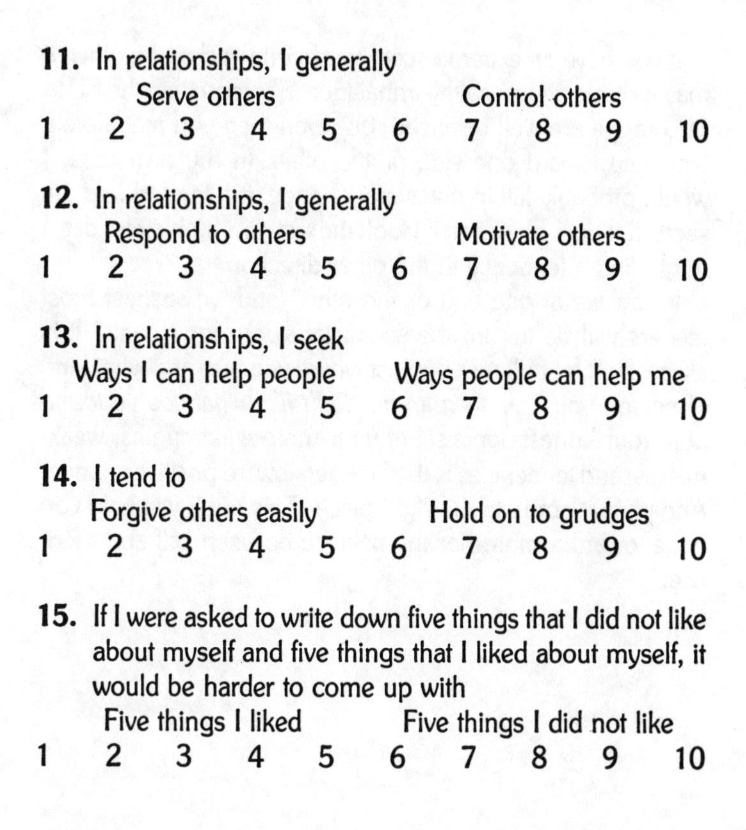

11. In relationships, I generally

Serve others — Control others

1 2 3 4 5 6 7 8 9 10

12. In relationships, I generally

Respond to others — Motivate others

1 2 3 4 5 6 7 8 9 10

13. In relationships, I seek

Ways I can help people — Ways people can help me

1 2 3 4 5 6 7 8 9 10

14. I tend to

Forgive others easily — Hold on to grudges

1 2 3 4 5 6 7 8 9 10

15. If I were asked to write down five things that I did not like about myself and five things that I liked about myself, it would be harder to come up with

Five things I liked — Five things I did not like

1 2 3 4 5 6 7 8 9 10

Scoring

Add the total of your circled scores and then find where you fall on the continuum between Sacrifice and Self. Put an "X" on the spot where you fall on the continuum.

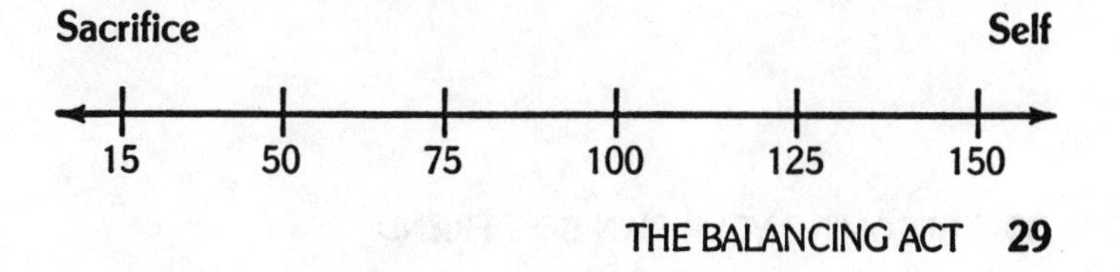

If you have an extreme score, far to one end or the other, it may indicate an unhealthy imbalance. Scores within the 50 to 100 range are well balanced, but even then you may note a tendency toward one side or the other. In my own case, I would probably fall in the average range, but tend toward the sacrificial side. However, if I took the test on a high-stress day, I might find a tendency in the other direction.

If you are at one end or the other (and we suspect most readers will be toward the sacrificial side), don't panic! It is always helpful to figure out just where you are, and what kind of person you are, *even if you don't like what you've found out.* Your honest appraisal of your motives, strengths, weaknesses, and tendencies is the first step toward positive change. And you've come to the right place. This book will help you edge toward a more healthy balance between self and sacrifice.

CHAPTER 3

Going Slowly

Your problem is not an inferiority complex. You see, you really are inferior!
—ZIGGY'S PSYCHIATRIST

Larry wanted to be my friend. I was a college senior helping out with a high-school youth group in a local church. Larry was the church's youth pastor. When it's your life calling to keep teenagers entertained and spiritually enlightened, you can go a bit crazy. Larry was no exception. He desperately needed a friend who was at least voting age—a colleague, a confidant, a pal. He decided that would be me.

So he started to hang out with me at the college. I did much of my socializing (and studying) in the college snack bar, and Larry would often show up for a cup of coffee with me. He would ask me probing personal questions, as if we were already best friends. He stopped short of being obnoxious, but I felt somewhat uncomfortable with him. I wanted to be nice. I respected his work with the youth group. But he was not my type of friend. I had not chosen to pal around with him. He had chosen me.

Yet he persisted.

It was his job, I figured. This was "relationship building" with a member of his volunteer staff.

His questions kept challenging me. His personal revelations and prayers kept pushing our acquaintance to a higher level. I gave him some leeway.

And a funny thing happened: We became friends. I began to feel more comfortable with the way he talked, the way he thought. I began to participate in what had been a one-way friendship. We counseled each other through some bumpy romances. We theorized and theologized. We shared ideas that helped both our careers.

As I look back, I realize that Larry affected my life in key ways at a crucial time. I am thankful for his friendship. I am glad he persisted.

Sometimes friendships just happen. You "click" with someone right away. But others, like mine with Larry, take time to get into. And all friendships take time to develop. You tell a best friend things that you'd never tell someone you just met at a party—no matter how well you've "clicked."

It's the same when you're becoming your own best friend.

It doesn't happen overnight. You have to learn to know yourself, to test yourself, to trust yourself. This can take some time.

Becoming your own best friend is like any other relationship—it takes time.

A guy goes to a psychologist and talks for an hour, pouring out his miserable feelings about his life, his family, but most of all, about himself.

The psychologist stands up at the end of the session and says, "You have poor self-esteem. That will be eighty-five dollars, please."

And the guy walks out of the office saying, "I should have known that."

This could be the beginning of a downward spiral for this patient. "Why did I just shell out eighty-five dollars to find out something I should have known myself? I'm just dumb, I guess. I can't figure these things out." The very *process* of trying to fix his self-esteem is taking away his self-esteem!

It can happen like that if you view poor self-esteem as a minor problem, requiring a slight adjustment. You can psyche yourself out. "Surely I should be able to like myself more," you might say. "It shouldn't be that hard!" But old habits die hard.

The sad fact is that *trying to improve your self-esteem can damage your self-esteem*. There's a circular logic that says, "If I were better I would feel better about myself. But I'm not, so I don't." If you have unrealistic expectations of how fast or how far you'll recover, your recovery will be stunted.

It does not happen all at once. It takes some time, and some trial and error. It's not a switch that you throw. It's not "Oh, I think I'll have a good self-esteem today." The long and winding road leading away from poor self-esteem is composed of many tiny steps.

Clearing Your Vision

When I first got contact lenses, I didn't pay attention to the cleansing regimen. I was haphazard about it, boiling them regularly but not always using the daily cleaner. As a result, deposits formed on the lenses that were essentially baked on. The lenses became blurry.

After a few months, I was telling a friend about my blurry lenses, and she asked, "Have you tried the enzymatic cleaner?"

I didn't even know there was such a thing, but I bought some. The first soaking improved the lenses a little. After a second soaking, they improved a bit more, and so on in the weeks that followed. I also was more careful in my regular cleaning, and so I was able to keep those lenses usable for several more months.

Self-esteem is like contact lenses.

Your sense of self is a lens through which you view the world, the people you deal with, and your own behavior. All the information that comes into your mind is processed through your sense of self.

People with different "lenses" see things differently. If you trip on the sidewalk, you may interpret that in various ways:

- "I'm so clumsy! I can't do anything right!"
- "Why can't they make these sidewalks straight? The town leaders obviously don't care about this part of town."
- "I'm lucky I didn't fall and seriously hurt myself."

If you have poor self-esteem, you are apt to see everything in that negative light. Your lenses are blurry. Whatever happens, on your mental picture you have superimposed the message "I am worthless." And the information you receive tends to confirm that message.

Even if you know you have poor self-esteem, and even if you grit your teeth and try to have better self-esteem, that "worthless" message is still there, being confirmed with your every action. It's like doing heat disinfection of contact lenses without cleaning them first. Those deposits get baked on.

You need the psychological equivalent of an enzymatic cleaner. Now, I'm no chemist, but I've learned enough from an eighth-grade lab and TV commercials to know that enzymes are reactive agents. They take apart a substance and break it down to its smallest components, essentially chewing it up for digestion. Deposits *collect*—they gather small particles into a mass that makes a lens blurry. Enzymes *tear apart* those particles, so they can be rinsed away.

Thus it is with poor self-esteem. Where did it come from? You may be able to identify precisely the person or event that sparked your self-esteem problems. Chances are, the problem started in your childhood, and for—how long? twenty, thirty, forty years?—you've been collecting deposits around that original cause.

To deal with poor self-esteem in an enzymatic way, we need to take it apart bit by bit. Success will not happen instantly, but the lenses will slowly clear up. You'll be able to see the world—and yourself within that world—more realistically.

Self-esteem is like contact lenses. Your sense of self is a lens through which you view the world, the people you deal with, and your own behavior.

The Magic Eyes

Lewis Smedes, in *Forgive and Forget,* tells a fable about hate, forgiveness, and new sight. A baker named Fouke caught his wife, Hilda, in adultery. Righteous man that he was, he pretended to forgive her, but deep inside he hated her for what she had done.

As the fable goes, every time he had a hateful thought toward Hilda, an angel came by and dropped a small pebble into Fouke's heart. This brought a stab of pain, which made Fouke hate Hilda all the more. And his heart grew heavier and heavier.

But then the angel told the baker how he could be healed. He needed the magic eyes. He needed to see Hilda "not as a wife who betrayed him, but as a weak woman who needed him."

Fouke protested that his wife was indeed guilty, and the angel agreed. But the past was past, the angel said. He needed to heal the hurt that was present. For this, he needed the magic eyes. But how would he get them?

"Only ask, desiring as you ask," the angel said, "and they will be given you. And each time you see Hilda through your new eyes, one pebble will be lifted from your aching heart."

It took a while, but finally the pain grew so great that Fouke asked for the magic eyes. He began to see his wife in a more favorable light. And one by one the pebbles were taken away. "He invited Hilda to come into his heart again," Smedes concludes, "and she came, and together they began again a journey into their second season of humble joy."

The story carries some deep truths. The pain we bear

from past hurts is great—and it can accumulate over the years. We cannot dump those pebbles all at once. It takes time. It takes the magic eyes.

I want you to see yourself as Fouke—*and as Hilda*. Whatever it is that you have not forgiven yourself for, I want you to ask for the magic eyes so that you can begin to see yourself as the beautiful (though sometimes weak) person you are.

Avoid the "Crash Course"

Dieting experts know this principle well. If you're, say, twenty pounds overweight, you *could* go on a crash program and perhaps lose it all in a week or two. But it would have devastating effects on your overall health—and you will probably gain the weight right back. Sudden success is usually short-lived.

No, the way to do it is to lose small increments of weight, a pound or two a week. You establish habits that you can maintain. It might frustrate you at first—all this work and only a pound or two lost. But six months later you will have reached your goal.

Recovering your self-esteem is something like that. The world is full of "crash courses" in asserting yourself. Everywhere you go, you meet people who are demanding their rights because that's what someone told them to do. They are all bluster and thunder—until they crash. (Maybe "crash course" is the right term after all.) When the hype is gone, they realize they still don't like themselves very much, and they might even be embarrassed about the ruckus they've caused.

Build your self-esteem a pound or two at a time. Get to the heart of it, the messages that form your personal doctrine about yourself, the habits you use to put yourself down, the fear of committing to yourself and stepping into life as a full human being. Isolate the villains that keep you bound, and deal with them one by one.

Persistence Pays

And even then you may slip back.

Sorry, I don't want to be a voice of doom, but you have to be ready for occasional slips. If you expect them and prepare for them, you won't slip back as far. The wise mountain climber anchors herself, tying herself to certain solid places. She expects some slips along the way and prepares for them. This way, she may lose a few meters but will not tumble down to the bottom. (I know nothing about mountain climbing, as you may have guessed. But the principle still makes sense.)

I spoke with a friend recently who has struggled for a long time with poor self-esteem. "I was doing really well," Amy said, "for about a year. But then there were some problems at work and I slipped back to square one."

She had gotten this new job about a year earlier, and it was a very positive development. Her previous job was a downer, but this one offered more money, more opportunities for advancement, and the people seemed friendlier. (Our employment situation can be a major factor, positive or negative, in our self-esteem.) And so she began "doing really well." She was out of an unhealthy romance, reestablishing good friendships, and making money.

But then she got ambushed by some problems at work. From my perspective, these weren't huge problems, personality conflicts mainly, but they took her by surprise and set her back—"to square one." Suddenly all the positives turned to negatives. She missed that old romance, she despaired of ever advancing in this job, and all her money seemed to go out the window to pay bills. Now she's thinking about getting a new job. If she does, I expect the cycle to continue. She'll ride the roller coaster up, up, up, and then plummet when a problem occurs.

Yet Amy didn't need to get knocked back to square one. If she had been ready for those problems at work, she could have dealt with them. She might have had a few dark nights of the soul, she might have lost a month or two on her recovery of self-esteem—but not a whole year.

Diane has a slightly different story. Two years ago she split up with her husband over his philandering (he had done so throughout their ten-year marriage). He disappeared, moving in with another woman in some mystery location, and Diane went through the divorce proceedings alone. (Though not entirely: she did have the support and encouragement of a group of friends from her church.) Occasionally, throughout this process, her husband would call and sweet-talk her. It was unclear what he wanted, but the calls were generally devastating to her.

Yet she has been steadily recovering her self-esteem, establishing a new single life for herself. She too got a new job and has been slowly dealing with the financial damage of the divorce.

She spoke to me the other day, unsure of what to do. Her divorce was final several months ago, but now her ex was in town and wanted to see her. He seemed sincere in wanting to pay for half of the divorce and to patch up old wounds—but he had always been an expert at *seeming* sincere. She didn't trust him.

Diane wanted to do the right thing. This might be an opportunity, she figured, to forgive him once and for all, to clear the past grudges out of her life so she could be emotionally free to start her life over. But she also worried that such a rendezvous might set her back, it might reopen old wounds.

As she talked to me, I could sense her frustration. She wanted to be further along. She wished that she could handle something like this with confidence and self-assuredness. But she knew she couldn't. She recognized her own weakness. I thought that was very wise, and I told her so.

When I'm sick, I get tired of it. You may know this feeling—sick and tired of being sick and tired. So, often I'll try to live as if I'm not sick. I'll pretend I'm healthy enough to go on about my normal business. But that just sets me up for a relapse, and more time in recovery than I otherwise would have needed.

Diane wanted to be "all better," fully recovered from her divorce and from the self-esteem issues that it dug up. But she wasn't there yet, and she knew it. I advised her not to see her former husband, not to set herself up for a fall.

In my work with people who are recovering from divorce, I often talk about that slippery slope. Like the mountain climber climbing the icy mountain, those in recovery may struggle to move forward a few steps, but they can also expect to slip back from time to time. If you expect those slips, they won't be so devastating. You can pick yourself up and move forward.

Self-esteem recovery, however, may even be worse, since poor self-esteem often begins in childhood. There might be some "time bombs" that go off as you journey toward wholeness—old ideas from parents or siblings or teachers or classmates that emerge again and again. These may knock you down for a while, but that does not mean you are doomed.

Amy needs to recognize that the slope toward wholeness is indeed slippery, but there are some footholds along the way. She has an "all or nothing" mentality that knocks her to the bottom of the slope whenever she starts to slip.

Diane has a better idea—ironically, because she more readily admits her own weakness. She knows she's not at the top of the slope yet, so she must be careful. And when she slips, she grabs for something to break her fall.

The slope toward wholeness is indeed slippery, but there are some footholds along the way.

Acting the Part

I am often surprised at the people who tell me they have poor self-esteem. On the surface, they are capable and confident, good friends with enjoyable personalities. But inside, they harbor deep feelings of self-doubt. To get along in the world, they have learned to be good actors. They show the public what it wants to see, and it works. They cope.

In some cases, this can be quite healthy. As a person pretends to be self-confident, he or she can take some risks and achieve some successes. When the person sees these victories occur, it can be a powerful encouragement:

"Hey, I guess I *can* do that." There's an old saying, "Clothes make the man," and sometimes it works that way with self-esteem. If you put on an external front of self-confidence, it *may* seep inside. You may actually convince yourself that you're worth something.

But in other cases, there's a dangerous division of personality. The coping mechanism backfires. On the outside, the person may find great success, but the inside message is "That's not me. If they knew the real me, they'd hate me." The person sets up a false image for public perusal, but even public victories become wounds to the real self within. The external success just mocks the internal sense of worthlessness. *They don't know the real me.*

What's the difference? In one case, the person maintains a connection with the "act," and in the other there's a separation. (It actually parallels two methods of stage-acting. One method seeks a unity between the actor and the character; the actor essentially brings out the part of himself that *is* the character. The other is all pretense; the actor becomes someone else.)

Sometimes people read self-esteem books to learn how to play this role. In the British comedy *Bedroom Farce,* one character regularly withdraws to give herself a pep talk: "I am confident and self-assured. I am in complete control." Of course, the rest of her behavior shows that she is anything but self-assured. Maybe that pep talk was giving that character the ammunition to face the rest of life. But maybe it was causing her to establish a false image of a confident self when she really should have been dealing with the issues in her life (and in the play) that were tearing her down.

This book is not about pep talks. We're not trying to show you how self-confident people act so that you can copy them. We're not asking you to pretend to have good self-esteem so you can achieve success in life. We're trying to help you uncover the value that you really *do* have. We're trying to help you identify the villains that have lied to you, and are still lying to you, about your own worth. We're pushing honesty, not play-acting. We don't want you to gloss over your faults, but neither do we want you to blindly accept assumptions about your shortcomings. We're giving you the tools to build a sturdy sense of your own self-worth, slowly but solidly.

I counseled a woman named Pat, who had recently seen her long-term relationship fall apart. She felt great pain and insecurity inside, but on the outside she put on an act. "I'm fine," she told her friends. "Everything's great." She went out partying, dancing, looking for a new relationship.

When I urged caution in seeking a new romance, she laughed it off. "I'm ready," she assured me. This was just a few weeks after her breakup.

Despite her attempts to mask her underlying feelings, I could tell that Pat was weak and vulnerable. She was unsure of herself, but desperately trying to prove to everybody (including herself) that she was still worth something. The quickest way to prove that, she apparently felt, was to land a new boyfriend. Which she did.

Which she shouldn't have.

The new relationship is unhealthy for Pat. I fear that she will be damaged by it, and that it will end even more painfully than her previous romance. But on the surface, she's fine. She's got somebody who says he loves her, and so she must be worth something, right?

Instead of taking the time to build a true, inner sense of self-esteem, she plays the game, she does the act, she grabs for the quick fix. But she's fooling herself. Her self-esteem is not fixed, and she'll soon be in another crisis situation.

Then there's Keith.

Keith's emotions took a tumble after his divorce. I talked with him about a year after his wife left him. He was in the pits, lethargic, in bad health, clinically depressed. Needless to say, his self-esteem was nowhere to be found.

"It's been a year now," he said. "I should be over this, shouldn't I?"

In addition to everything else, he felt guilty because he was not recovering as fast as he thought he should be. And he worried that something must *really* be wrong with him.

I assured Keith that, in my work with divorce recovery, it regularly took two years, sometimes three to five, before someone was "over" it. That slippery slope is not crested easily.

Keith smiled. I realized that this simple fact was a healing touch. I had said the same thing to Pat—don't expect to get over this overnight. She had rejected it, but Keith was ready to accept this truth. In fact, it changed his whole outlook. Oh, he was still in the pits, but not doomed to stay there. Now he knew he was still on schedule. He would heal—in time.

Many who suffer from poor self-esteem feel strangely guilty about that. "I know I should have more confidence, but I just can't." If nothing else, this book should ease that guilt. There are reasons for the way you feel. Let's identify them and deal with them. Let's get started on that long, slow road to health.

CHAPTER 4

Taking Stock of Yourself

Know thyself.
—SOCRATES

He who knows others is learned;
He who knows himself is wise.
—LAO-TSE

"I can't think of anything."

Christine was drawing a blank. She was gazing up into the corner of her mind that holds memories, and she couldn't find what she was looking for.

This was not a counseling session. Christine was an old friend, and I had been crowing about some recent accomplishment of mine, when I suddenly realized I was dominating the conversation. So I had tried to draw her out. "Tell me about something good that you've done recently," I asked. "Yes, what's the best thing you've done in the last week?"

"I—I don't know," she stammered.

"All right," I said. "The last year."

Still nothing.

"All right. Your whole life. Tell me about something good you have done in your life."

She still just gazed upward and came back empty-handed. "I can't think of anything," she shyly admitted.

"Come on," I urged, "there has to be something!"

The spark of a memory came to her. "When I was in junior high, our group took some disadvantaged kids on a hayride. I helped organize it. That was pretty good, I guess."

I assure you, this was not the only deed of charity or quality she had done in her life. But somehow she had erased the good things from her memory, or relabeled them, or put them so far back that they were hard to reach. When she thought of herself, she did not see the kind helper who gave a bunch of underprivileged kids the ride of their lives. No, she saw someone who struggled with various things in her life—romance, family, career plans.

As we talked, I learned that she wrote poetry. I begged her to read some to me, and I thought it was pretty good. I also knew that she had done some acting in amateur theater, and was pretty good at this, too. She was clever, fun to be with, and I told her so. My words were like revelations to her. Surely she knows this about herself already, I thought. But it seemed that she had never been properly introduced—to herself.

Roger was in our singles' group and I guess you could say he was a bit of a misfit. In social situations he just didn't know how to act, and at times people made fun of him behind his back.

When Sam befriended Roger, none of us thought it

would really last. They started by just talking together and spending time together now and then. This evolved into ballgames, fishing trips, and eventually joint vacations. I thought Sam just felt sorry for Roger at first, and perhaps at first that's all it was. But when I asked Sam about Roger, he seemed genuinely interested and definitely caring. I was impressed by his dedication to Roger.

The results were most dramatic for Roger, although I'm sure both he and Sam benefited from the interaction. Little by little Roger seemed to become more aware of social cues. He grew in his social skills and in his sense of humor. He was able to laugh and joke with others, and in time he became integrated into the social structure of the group. He was still viewed as being a little different, but he was liked and accepted by others. The biggest difference was the fact that Roger had changed. His personality was basically the same, but he was now more socially aware. He knew himself. And he could see how he came across to others. Sam had taught him how others viewed some of his behaviors, and had guided him in his behavior. Roger's blind spots were enlightened, and he was able to laugh at himself and enjoy the group.

Knowing yourself means coming to terms with both strengths and weaknesses. If you suffer from poor self-esteem, it is likely that you are overlooking some of your strengths. But you might also be shying away from examining specific weak areas. It's easier to say "I'm just no good" than to pinpoint exactly what you're dissatisfied with. If you did, why, then you might have to work on improving some of these things.

The Johari Window

In graduate school I picked up a helpful model known as the Johari Window (see fig. 4.1). It may sound like an exotic Eastern artifact, but actually it's named that because the two men who first developed the idea were named Joe and Harry.

	Known to self	Unknown to self
Known to others	A	B
Unknown to others	C	D

Figure 4.1. The Johari Window.

A This section represents areas of our life that are known to us and known to others. These include information that is considered common knowledge: where we live, where we work, and so on. It also includes our self-expression—aspects of our personality we freely share with others.

B This section represents areas of our life that are known to others that we are not aware of. Sometimes these are known as "blind spots." Our friends may think we're selfish, but we might have no idea they feel that way. When people "talk behind our backs," we're in area B. In

Christine's case it was reversed—others knew good things about her that she wasn't accepting.

C This section represents areas of our life that are known to us but unknown to others. This area includes our secrets. We may know that our motives are selfish in regard to a particular friend, but we might act in a very giving way in order to win that person's favor. Our true motives are known to us, but unknown to others. Many who suffer from addictions live in area C. They try to hide their problems from others. This is also true of some who feel ashamed about incidents from their past.

D This section represents areas of our life that are yet undiscovered. This includes all those things that are true of us, but that others don't know, and in fact we don't know, either. This is uncharted territory. These are the places we haven't yet dared to go. Some call these unconscious motives, behaviors, or thoughts, such as the woman who fears dogs but has no recollection of the bite she suffered at two years of age.

Many people's lives look like figure 4.2, especially if their self-image is out of balance.

You'll notice that the smallest area is A, or the information about us that is known to others and to ourselves. We are very closed and quite unaware. In such cases, the areas for blind spots (B) and secrets (C) tend to be larger. We are guarded, private, and unaware of how others perceive us. We probably do not have healthy, intimate friendships.

But as we discover ourselves, facing up to our strengths and weaknesses, and as we open up in honesty to our closest friends, our Johari Window begins to look more like figure 4.3.

You can see from the window that the area known to

	Known to self	Unknown to self
Known to others	A	B
Unknown to others	C	D

Figure 4.2. Johari Window for a person who knows little about self and about whom others know little.

	Known to self	Unknown to self
Known to others	A	B
Unknown to others	C	D

Figure 4.3. Johari Window for a person who knows much about self and about whom others know much.

self and others is now the largest. We are open and honest with others, and in the process we learn a lot about ourselves from our friends. Now the smallest area is D. We have far less that is hidden from ourselves and others. The unconscious has become conscious and the secrets have been brought out into the open. It is noteworthy that areas B, C, and D will never disappear, and indeed they should not. We never get to the point where everything about us becomes public. Some things will always be private. In addition, we will never know everything that others think about us because there are things that they should keep to themselves. There will always be some things that will never be known (D). But the more intimate our friendships, and the more secure we are with ourselves, the more that is revealed to us.

As you share yourself with others, you will deepen your friendships and at the same time learn more about yourself.

Getting to Know Yourself

I've talked about the fact that self-esteem recovery does not occur overnight. Instead, there are steps along a lengthy road. In this book, we'll offer ten specific steps to get you started. I urge you to dig in and do these things. Don't just read them.

The road starts here, with self-knowledge. It's one thing to say, with Socrates, "Know thyself." It's quite another to figure out how. We'll start with a personal inventory.

Step 1: Make a Personal Inventory of Pluses and Minuses.

There are several ways to get to know yourself better, how people perceive you, and what your strengths and weaknesses are. I would recommend that you start by "self-reporting." List your own strengths and weaknesses as you perceive them. Consider not only your physical appearance, but also your mental ability, social skills, work habits, personality, relationships, and spiritual gifts. (For future use, as you write them down, put a plus sign in front of the strengths and a minus sign in front of the weaknesses.)

Physical Appearance. This is certainly not the most important aspect of who you are, but it's the most obvious, so let's start here. Get your pen and paper ready and start jotting down your good and bad features. Be honest with yourself—what are *you* happy with and not happy with?

Mental Ability. Are you as smart as you'd like to be? Are there certain subjects in which you have expertise? Are there other areas you'd like to know more about? Remember that researchers have found at least seven different kinds of intelligence. You may have a poor memory, but great analytical skills, or vice versa. Are you a creative soul? Do you come up with crazy ideas? How's your attention span? Do you read a lot?

Social Skills. How do you function in groups? Are you generally aware of the needs of others? Do you have a certain role in the groups you're a part of? Often, groups have unofficial roles—one may be a leader, another an assistant, another a grabber of new people, another a questioner. What's your role? Do you listen well? Do you care about people and/or pray for them? Do you remember people's names? Do you communicate well?

Work Habits. How well do you do what you do? Are you conscientious in your work? Do you try to earn your pay through hard work? How do you treat your co-workers? Do you help to create a good working environment? Are you fair to your boss? Do you complain a lot? Do you come up with good ideas on the job?

Personality. Do you have a good sense of humor? Are you too dependent on others? Too independent? Are you warm and friendly? Are you too shy? Do you get mad easily? Or do you wish you stood up for yourself more? Are you honest? Loyal? Responsible? Scatterbrained? Shallow? Fake? Do you generally treat others as you would like to be treated?

Relationships. Are you loyal to family and friends? Do you communicate well with your family? If you have kids, what do you do well as a parent? What don't you do well? Do you provide for them? Do you clean up after them? If you are married, how good a spouse are you? Are you understanding and challenging, accessible and giving? If you are single, do you tend to throw yourself into unwise relationships? Or do you have good taste in friends and romantic partners? In general, do you keep in touch with friends? Do you make new friends easily?

Spiritual Gifts. If you are a Christian, have you thought about how God has specially gifted and empowered you? Are you using your gifts in effective ways? Do you encourage others spiritually? Do you find it easy to develop a spiritual kinship with others? Do you feel that you are growing spiritually? Do you observe certain spiritual disciplines, such as regular prayer, meditation, or Bible reading?

Reports from Others

It might be helpful to compare notes with someone else. Is there a close friend or relative you feel you can trust with your self-assessment, perhaps a spouse or parent (but not necessarily)? Consider going through your list with this person to see if he or she agrees.

This area of self-evaluation reminds me of a poem that was written by my grandfather, Charles V. Whiteman, a man who never got past the eighth grade. He was disabled in his work, so he led a difficult life, eking out a living with his little farm. He was loved and respected by many, and left behind thousands of poems that are his legacy of uncommon wisdom.

Check Up on Yourself

An errand boy for a mercantile firm,
  Was sent on an errand one day;
And while returning stopped in at the store
  Of a neighbor's, not far away.

He called his employer, but changed his voice,
  And applied for a job in his store;
He said he was well qualified for the job,
  As he'd often run errands before.

His employer told him he had a good boy,
In fact one that couldn't be beat;
The boy thanked him kindly and hung up the phone,
And started once more for the street.

"Hold on," said the merchant, "just what do you mean,
You impertinent, fresh, little elf?"
"Not a thing," said the boy in a courteous tone,
"I was just checking up on myself."

"I think I'm all right," the boy then explained,
"But maybe there's some won't agree,
And that was my method of finding out,
Just what my boss thinks of me."

His sensible logic should be helpful to all,
Though perhaps we would get a surprise
If instead of our self-pride we'd all try to find,
How we stand in other folks' eyes.

I think it a very good notion, don't you?
To put self-esteem on the shelves;
And occasionally find what the world thinks of us—
Like the boy, check up on ourselves.

—Charles V. Whiteman

Personality Tests

Another way to measure your personality is through one of the many available personality tests. The Myers-Briggs Personality Test, the Taylor–Johnson Personality Test, the "DISC" Personal Profile System—any of these can give you interesting insights into the way you are, and the way others are. Frequently we judge ourselves for being, say, too emotional when everyone around us is thinking objectively. Tests like these reveal that there are different personality types.

There's another very simple test I have taken, which I've remembered for years because of the visual images it evokes. It is not nearly as sophisticated as the others, but I've never seen a test more user-friendly. It comes from a book by Gary Smalley and John Trent—*The Two Sides of Love*. With their permission, I present it here. (If you want a more complete explanation as to its interpretation, I highly recommend their book.)

THE SMALLEY–TRENT PERSONAL STRENGTHS SURVEY*

Read the adjectives in the four boxes, and then circle each word or phrase that seems to describe you. Don't try to analyze or outthink the test. It only provides a superficial overview of your basic tendencies.

Next, add up the number of items you circled in each box. Then double your score to come up with a total for each box. Take your total scores and put them on the graph provided. Connect the dots in order to get a visual idea of your personality type.

Remember, the test will only be helpful if you are honest. There is no advantage to trying to make yourself seem better or worse than you really feel.

Interpretation of the Test

Smalley and Trent use animal images to describe these four personality types.

L		B	
Take charge	Bold	Deliberate	Discerning
Determined	Purposeful	Controlled	Detailed
Assertive	Decision maker	Reserved	Analytical
Firm	Leader	Predictable	Inquisitive
Enterprising	Goal driven	Practical	Precise
Competitive	Self-reliant	Orderly	Persistent
Daring	Adventurous	Factual	Scheduled
"Let's do it now!"		"How was it done in the past?"	
Double number circled ___		**Double number circled ___**	

O		G	
Takes risks	Fun-loving	Loyal	Adaptable
Visionary	Likes variety	Undemanding	Sympathetic
Motivator	Enjoys change	Even keel	Thoughtful
Energetic	Creative	Avoids conflict	Nurturing
Very verbal	Group oriented	Enjoys routine	Patient
Promoter	Mixes easily	Dislikes change	Tolerant
Avoids details	Optimistic	Deep relationships	Good listener
"Trust me! It'll work out."		"Let's keep things the way they are."	
Double number circled ___		**Double number circled ___**	

Lions (L) are leaders. They are often the bosses at work. They express a take-charge attitude, especially when it comes to problem-solving. Smalley and Trent say these people are "doers, not watchers or listeners." And in their discussion of

Personal Strengths Survey Chart

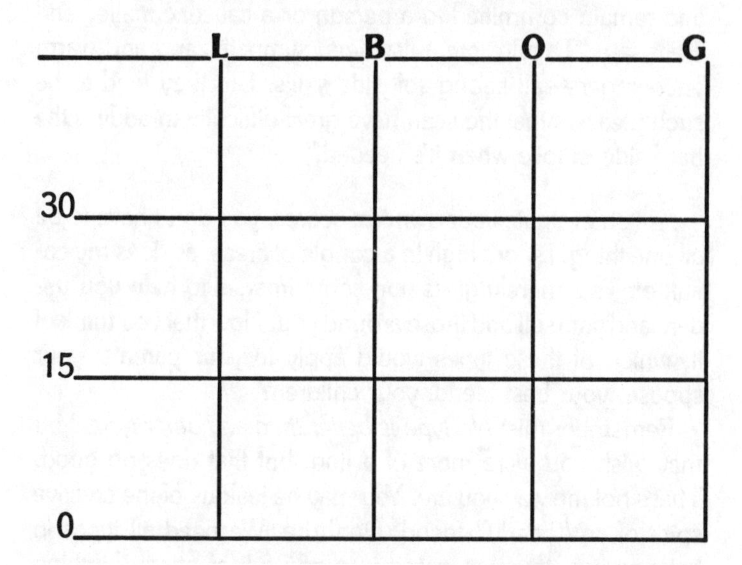

the "hard" side of love and the "soft" side, lions show the hard side and might need some softening up.

Beavers (B) are hard workers who like things done right. These people, the authors say, "actually read instruction manuals!" They have standards and rules, and thus tend to be steady, dependable people. They too express the "hard" side of love, and might have to learn to break the rules for a good purpose.

Otters (O) are playful types, creative and expressive. They tend to be talkative and outgoing—"people" people. They usually need to be liked—and this places them on the "soft" side of love, letting things go that maybe shouldn't be overlooked.

Golden Retrievers (G) are—pardon the pun—doggedly

loyal. They can absorb a great amount of pain and frustration and remain committed to a person or a cause. Smalley and Trent say, "They're great listeners, sympathizers, and warm encouragers—all strong soft-side skills. But they tend to be such pleasers that they can have great difficulty in adding the hard side of love when it's needed."

As you evaluate your own test scores, you don't have to be all one thing. I score high in a couple of areas, as does my co-author. This merely gives you some images to help you understand yourself and those around you. Now that you think of it, which of these types would apply to your parents, your spouse, your best friend, your children?

Remember this: *No type is better than any other type*. You may wish you were more of a lion, but that does no good. That's not the way you are. You may be jealous of the creative spirit of an "otterly" friend. Don't be. We need all types to balance out. Imagine going to a zoo full of otters. Nothing else, just otters. That gets old after a while. Any business, any church, any home needs all types to function smoothly.

And notice the balanced treatment each type gets in this interpretation. Each type has a host of good things—leadership, consistency, creativity, loyalty. But each type also has weaknesses—nonlistening, inflexibility, people-pleasing, codependency. Every person has strengths and weaknesses. Healthy living comes from using your strengths and working on your weaknesses.

At the end of this book is an Appendix with two tests that you can take. The first is a Personal Style Analysis and the second a Personal Interests and Values Survey. Both tests

take about ten minutes to complete. Feel free to photocopy these tests, fill them in, and then mail them to our offices. For a fee, we will mail you a six-page computer analysis of your personality style, or your interests and values, or both.

Step 2: Begin to Compliment Yourself in the Presence of Others.

How often do you say negative things about yourself in front of others? Probably more often than you think.

"Oh, I could never do that."

"I wish I looked as good as she does."

"I'm just no good at that sort of thing."

"Sorry, I'm just not in top form today."

Most of us share our self-doubts and limitations rather easily. But do we ever say positive things about ourselves? Not often.

"I enjoy doing that because I think I do it pretty well."

"That turned out nicely, if I do say so myself."

"I love wearing this outfit because it makes me look good."

"I am so thankful that God gave me the ability to do this."

You seldom hear this sort of thing. Why? For social reasons, mostly. Many of us have been taught that it's rude to praise yourself, and that it's much more polite, even attractive, to put yourself down. There is a *little* bit of truth in this, but we need to sort through it carefully.

What's So Bad About Pride?

Humility is good. It is good to recognize your limits. Conversely, it is bad to think too highly of yourself. Pride is dangerous. Why? What's so bad about pride?

Pride Is Comparative. Pride says, "I am better than everyone else." Thus, a proud statement is an attack on others. Humility understands that all people are precious and that each person has individual gifts that are valuable.

Pride Is Isolating. Pride says, "I am self-sufficient. I don't need anyone else. I got here on my own merit. I don't need other people. I don't need God." Humility understands that we need each other. Whatever deeds we may accomplish, we probably owe a great deal to many other people, and we certainly owe a lot to God.

Pride Is Out of Balance. Pride says, "Because I have done this one thing (say, getting the winning hit in a softball game), I am great in every aspect of my life." Humility understands that every person has strengths and weaknesses, and keeps a balanced sense of self.

Positive Response

But how highly *should* we think of ourselves? As we come to a balanced understanding of who we are, with our strengths and weaknesses, can we share that with others? Can we compliment ourselves in a wholesome way—not comparing, not isolating, not out of balance, not "exalting" ourselves, but just responding positively to who we are or what we have done? I think so. Here are some strategies you might employ.

Start with an Understanding Friend. Find someone who understands what you're doing. Explain "I'm trying to improve my self-esteem and I need to compliment myself in the presence of someone else. You're that 'someone else,' okay?"

Make Balanced Statements. Say "I'm no good at basketball, but I'm a great badminton player." You can preserve your sense of humility with the negative statement while you affirm yourself with the positive.

Thank God for Your Success. If God is important in your life, obviously you owe him the credit for the good things you have done. But you still need to acknowledge that a good thing was done. "That church dinner I organized really came off well. I thank God for keeping me focused enough to do the planning."

Ask for a Compliment—And Accept It. This is something you can do with a close friend that you probably can't do with a casual acquaintance. Say "I'm working on my self-esteem, and I need to accept a compliment from someone. Can you think of anything good to say about me?" It's not exactly complimenting *yourself,* but it's the same idea. As you accept the compliment, you are affirming something good about yourself.

A best friend doesn't always heap praise on you. But a best friend usually knows when you need a kind word. A best friend delivers accurate, honest compliments to build you up when you need it most. As you become a best friend to yourself, you can do the same.

Step 3: Isolate a Problem in Your Life and Take Steps to Correct It.

One of the biggest lies we tell ourselves is that we will never change, that we will always be stupid or ugly or nerdy or fill in the blank. It is true that there are *some* things we cannot change about ourselves, but we can change other things.

For this step I want to borrow two big ideas from the recovery movement, most notably Alcoholics Anonymous. The first is the application of the Serenity Prayer: "God grant me the serenity to accept the things I cannot change, the courage to change the things I can, and the wisdom to know the difference." A key step in our self-evaluation is to divvy up the things we can change about ourselves and the things we can't.

The second big recovery idea I'll borrow is "One day at a time." I'll adapt it to "One project at a time." Don't be overwhelmed by your list of weaknesses. Choose one and work on it. It might take a month, or two, or twelve, but you should see some improvement. Then you can choose another weakness and work on that.

Making the List and Checking It Twice

Go back to your list of strengths and weaknesses. We'll focus on the weaknesses now. Read through it and reevaluate these in light of the personality test you took in step 1. Is there anything that you've realized is not a weakness at all, but just the way you are? If you felt bad because you're a golden retriever and not a lion, but now you realize it's okay to be a golden retriever, you can cross those golden-retriever qualities (or the lack of lion qualities) off your weakness list. Be honest, and if you still feel there's a weakness there, leave it on. But go carefully through your weaknesses and put an "X" over the minus sign of any you're tossing off the list.

Now go through the list again and find those weaknesses that you really can't do anything about. They're out of your control. Many physical attributes are like this—height, or facial features, or some scar or birthmark—as well as some physical abilities. Put a circle around the minus sign for each of these weaknesses. These are things you will just have to live with. I'm not saying that's easy, but it would be futile to try to change them. Pray for the serenity to accept them.

You're left with weaknesses that you feasibly could do something about. Let's grade these in terms of the amount of effort necessary to change them. How hard would it be to change this tendency or that trait or some habit? Put an "A" beside those that would be easiest to change, a "B" beside those requiring moderate effort, and a "C" beside those that are hardest. Just make your best guess about the difficulty you'd face.

Now limit your scope to those weaknesses you have labeled with an "A." Choose one to start working on this week. That's right, we're starting with the easiest. You need to establish some success in self-improvement before you tackle the tough stuff.

Focusing on this one weak area, you now need to come up with your *plan.* Let me offer some suggestions.

Set Measurable and Attainable Goals. How will you know when you have succeeded? Come up with a specific measurement, but keep it reasonable.

Set a Specific Action a Week at a Time. So what are you going to *do* about it? You don't need to set a year's worth of actions; let one lead you to the next.

Give Yourself Specific Messages. Write down a message that may serve as a brief pep talk. Memorize this message. Or plant it in "time bomb" places where you'll see it—a mirror, a refrigerator, on the TV.

Consider Accountability. Don't rush this if you're uncomfortable with it, but it will help you greatly if you can ask a friend to check up on you. If you know you have to answer to someone else, you will have more motivation to follow through. This can put stress on a friendship, however, so make sure your relationship is strong enough to handle it.

As you work on your weaknesses, watch out for the mindset that says "Once I take care of these things, *then* I'll be worth something." You're worth a lot already. All of us have strengths and weaknesses. None of us is perfect. By working toward improvement, you're not grasping for some value that you presently lack, you're just demonstrating the value you already have. And you're demonstrating this mostly to yourself.

CHAPTER 5

Finding the Villains

We forfeit three-fourths of ourselves to be like other people.
—ARTHUR SCHOPENHAUER (1788–1860)

When I brought home my report card, I was so proud of my all A's and only one B. It was the best I had ever done. But my enthusiasm was crushed when my dad's only comment was, "Next time let's bring up that B."
—A RESPONDENT TO OUR SURVEY

Step 4: Identify the "Villains" That Have Damaged Your Self-Esteem.

Let's say your friends suddenly start avoiding you. You notice that everyone keeps a distance. The ones you used to pal around with are now not available. You get a cold shoulder from people you have not wronged. What do you do?

You might go to your best friend and ask, "What's the

problem?" (That's what friends are for; they'll tell you what you need to hear.)

Let's say your friend responds, "Well, I heard that you thought you were better than the rest of us. I heard that you were bad-mouthing all your friends."

"That's not true!" you protest. "Where did you hear that?"

And so your friend gives you the name of someone else, who refers you to someone else who heard it from someone else. Eventually, you trace the false rumor to its source, Nosy Nora.

"How could you spread a rumor like that, Nora?" you challenge. "You know it's not true!"

Nora looks sheepish and says, "Remember last week when we were talking? You said you had gone way past everyone else and that they didn't know anything and you knew it all."

"Huh?" you wonder, and then it dawns on you. "No, Nora. I was telling about a party I went to, and a bunch of friends were following me in their cars because they didn't know where the place was. A stoplight turned red behind me and they had to stop, but I didn't realize it, so I went way past everyone else and they didn't know how to get there, because I was the only one who knew the way. You misunderstood."

"Oops," says Nora. "Sorry."

There are rumors going around in your head about your own value.

"I'm no good."

"I'm not smart enough."

"I'm not pretty enough."

"I can't make friends."

You've heard them, haven't you? But where did they come from? When did you first get this message and put it in your personal doctrine? It may take some digging to find the source of this errant message. That's why counselors spend so much time reviewing your past. If you find out where the problems started, you may be able to fix them at their root.

There are false rumors about you going around in your head. It's important that you try to determine where they came from.

A friend of mine, in his thirties, recently told me a story about roller skating. He had never really learned to skate, but a friend dragged him to a skating rink and he tried it. He actually did okay on the straightaway, he said, but the rink has this nasty way of curving at both ends. He spent much of his time on the floor as ten-year-olds whirled (and break-danced!) around him.

"Why didn't you ever learn to skate?" I asked him.

"I have weak ankles," he answered, but then he stopped short, digging up a distant memory.

"No!" he said, surprising me with his forcefulness. "I don't have weak ankles! Now that I think about it, I've never had problems with twisted or sprained ankles. But when I was seven, my mom told me that I had bad ankles and I've believed it ever since.

"That's right," he said, summoning the memory. "I was at a skating rink for the first time, and having trouble keeping my balance. I mean, I was a clumsy kid. My ankles may have been fine, but the rest of me was a real klutz. And mom was trying to reassure me. 'You must have weak ankles,' she said in a loving way. 'So do I.' I mean, she wasn't trying to put me down or anything. If anything, she was trying to give me an excuse so I wouldn't feel so klutzy. But because of that, for the rest of my life I have assumed I could not skate because of my weak ankles."

A seed planted by an important person in your childhood can become a choking vine when you're an adult.

Rest assured, my friend is not emotionally scarred because of this ankle thing. At worst, he lost out on a few teen skating parties. But this is a minor example of something that becomes major in many people's lives—maybe in yours, too.

The Usual Suspects

Natural Frustration

It's not hard to see how a child begins to see herself as inadequate. Children are too short, too weak, too dumb, and not old enough. At least that's the message they often receive. Some of this natural frustration can be overcome with a great deal of encouragement, but the fact remains: children are still growing and learning. They need help doing many things. We cannot entrust them with adult responsibilities. They do not know as much as older people. Some feelings of inadequacy can sink in during these developmental years.

Society in General

This is another pervasive villain (so much so that we devote chapter 8 to it). As children grow, they are bombarded with messages from the media and from other institutions. Many of these messages say, "You're not good enough, pretty enough, smart enough, savvy enough."

Well-meant comments are often taken wrongly. They serve to confirm our self-doubts, and thus become part of our personal doctrine. "I am fat. Aunt Ethel said so."

Misunderstandings

But there are other specific situations that often shatter self-esteem. Your sense of inadequacy might stem from an innocent comment that you misunderstood. "Don't you look big in that dress!" Aunt Ethel may have been trying to compliment you back then when you were eleven, but you were already feeling uneasy about gaining weight, and so you've thought of yourself as fat ever since.

We go through times of severe sensitivity while growing up, especially during puberty. Our bodies seem out of control, and always too big or too little—we can't win. We begin to sense our sexuality, and we feel guilty about that. With pimples on our faces, braces on our teeth, and a million flawless models on TV, we feel ugly anyway. So all it takes is an unthinking aunt or an unsubtle friend to wound us deeply.

In such an environment, well-meant comments are often taken wrongly. They serve to confirm our self-doubts and thus become part of our personal doctrine. "I am fat. Aunt Ethel said so." Of course she said no such thing, but we think she did, and so the damage is done. Through the years, we amass a body of evidence to corroborate Aunt Ethel's charge. Most of this evidence is flimsy and circumstantial, but it doesn't take much to build a case against ourselves.

We build on misunderstandings of the past. We can be convinced of some grievous shortcomings that don't exist.

We need to go back, as much as we can, and dig out those foundations of our misunderstandings. We need to reconstruct our personal history.

We can learn a lesson from the former Soviet Union. History books in the Soviet bloc were full of the glorious exploits of Lenin and Stalin. Anything negative was ruled out. But with the fall of communism, historians have been allowed to go back and take an honest look at what happened. They are literally reconstructing their history, challenging the lies that formed a foundation for their national identity, and forging a new identity.

That's the kind of reconstruction we need to do. It's not easy. In some cases, it's not entirely possible. But if we can challenge those early misunderstandings about our own value and try to reconstruct a personal history based on truth, we will be healthier.

If we can challenge those early misunderstandings about our own value and try to reconstruct a personal history based on truth, we will be healthier.

Perhaps you can trace an aspect of your low self-esteem to someone else misunderstanding you. I remember once as a boy I said something positive about myself and a friend thought I was being stuck up. I wasn't! I was merely commenting on the satisfaction of something I had done well. But it was the worst thing in the world to be conceited. Because my friend misunderstood me, I refrained from saying anything good about myself for a long time.

Childhood is a time of learning to communicate. Most of us learn the language quickly, but there's a host of additional communication factors that we take longer to learn—tone of voice, body language, subtext, desired response. Younger children don't know how they come across to others, and they don't really care. That's why they "say the darnedest things." Older kids slowly learn how to understand others and be understood.

A friend of mine directs plays at a high school. His casts run the gamut from 12 to 18 years of age. He says it's fascinating to see how they work. The younger ones tend to be more self-absorbed—either shy or flamboyant, but in their own worlds. The older ones connect better with others. They've learned to communicate.

The point is that misunderstandings regularly occur at young ages. We're all still learning to read each other! The problem is that so many elements of our "personal doctrine" are adopted at those early ages—and they're often based on those misunderstandings.

We need to go back, in our own memories, and forgive those misunderstandings. We need to renounce their hold on us. It would be silly for me to keep from expressing satisfaction with my own work merely because Billy Evans thought I was stuck up when we were both 12.

Competition

Another common villain is competition. It's a dog-eat-dog world out there—especially when you're six and your brother is eight. In a family, siblings fight for attention, for love, for identity. Wise parents spread their affection evenly, but it can quickly become a situation in which Bobby's victory is Sally's loss.

Competition also occurs in classrooms and on playing fields. Schoolmates fight for the same love and attention, from peers and classmates. Kids can be meticulous list-makers. "I'm the fourth best ballplayer" or "I'm the sixth best looking." When dating time comes around, the competition intensifies. Who gets whom? Who wins whom? Winners dance the night away as losers sulk.

Children who are otherwise very sweet can become tigers when competing with siblings or classmates. They may not mean to be cruel, but they are fighting for their lives. I mean that almost literally—they are fighting for their identities. In the competitive world of growing up, if you are somebody, then I am nobody—so I'll do what I can to make you a nobody, so I can be a somebody. It's a zero-sum game of success and failure.

Those wounds run deep. There are betrayals by friends, put-downs by brothers and sisters—and believe me, these people know exactly where to stab you.

One of my clients, Ray, told me of a time when he shut his sister out of his life. Ray idolized his older brother, a strong, silent type, and tried to mimic him in many ways. His sister Kim, three years younger, was outgoing and talented, always showing off. In his high school years, Ray says, he was a nice guy with many friends, caring and

well-respected. But he pointedly ignored his sister, who longed for his approval.

Kim idolized Ray the way Ray idolized the older brother, but Ray was afraid of her, and so he shut her out. (Ray surprised himself as he began to figure this out.) Ray was torn between his brother's model of quiet confidence and his sister's flamboyant expression of her talent. He was afraid that he would lose himself if he identified too much with Kim. If he maintained the quiet attitude he respected so much in his brother, he would be overshadowed by the way Kim showed off—he'd just be "Kim's brother." But if he competed with Kim, showing off his own talents, he would fail to live up to his older brother's example. His solution: Ignore her. He remembers times when she would camp out at his locked door, saying, "Open up, Ray, I want to talk," and he'd only mutter, "Go away."

What must that have done to her self-esteem? Fortunately, this only lasted a few years, years in which Ray's identity was especially fragile. Later, Ray and Kim became great friends. But Ray was a "villain" in Kim's life for a time. He had his reasons, as we've seen. He was struggling to maintain his own identity. But he was unusually cruel to her in the process, and her sense of identity may still bear some of the scars.

So when we seek out the "villains" in our own lives, we are not saying, "You are an evil person." We are merely saying, "You have damaged me." They may have had their reasons. Maybe they had to do what they did.

Twisted Discipline

In many cases, parents or teachers damage a child's self-esteem through what we might call twisted discipline.

That is, they have the idea that the way to raise a child is to break a child. If you praise a child too much, they think, the child gets lazy or too proud. You must keep challenging your children by criticizing their work, their appearance, their intelligence.

Of course that way of thinking is dead wrong. There is a place for challenge in child-rearing, but not at the expense of a child's sense of self-worth. Praise is crucial. And yet many parents, trying to be good parents, have robbed their children of self-esteem.

The myriad talk shows on daytime TV can be pretty crazy, but they often provide an interesting glimpse of our nation's psychological condition. Occasionally you'll see people facing off with their parents, telling the world everything that went wrong, with Sally or Oprah or Geraldo and their studio audiences playing shrink. I've seen these adult children detailing their parents' insults:

"You never once told me I looked nice. It was always, 'Wouldn't you look better in the red dress?'"

"You yelled at me whenever I didn't hit a home run. I was afraid to swing the bat."

"You always picked on my boyfriends. It was like I didn't have the sense to pick someone good."

And usually the parental response is the same: "It was for your own good. I was trying to do what was best for you."

The dysfunctional-family musical *Into the Woods* has an insightful exchange between Rapunzel and her mother, the Witch. Rapunzel enters whimpering and the Witch asks what's wrong. "Oh, nothing!" the daughter replies, and proceeds to list her woes—the Witch had locked her in a tower for years, blinded the prince who found her, cut her fabulous hair and sent her off to the desert.

"Because of the way you treated me," Rapunzel concludes, "I'll never, *never* be happy!"

The Witch looks at her troubled daughter and says, "I was just trying to be a good mother."

It's funny because it's so close to the truth. Parenting is a tough business. Mothers and fathers don't always know what to do. They may have some wacky idea that self-esteem is a threat, that a child with a healthy self-image will not be obedient or submissive. They may be fighting with their own poor self-esteem, and thus have no idea how to build positive self-esteem in a child. They may do all sorts of bad parenting in an effort to do good parenting. And the children may bear the scars.

Parents teach their children the answers to two crucial questions: Am I important? Are others important? The combination of these two questions results in four distinct parenting styles, as we see in figure 5.1.

Are Others Important?

Am I Important?	Others are not valued	Others are valued
Self is valued	Free style of parenting No structure Creates self-esteem without a social context Fosters selfishness	Healthy parenting Reasonable structure Creates self-esteem in a social context Fosters self-sacrifice with appropriate boundaries
Self is not valued	Dysfunctional parenting No structure or inconsistent structure Creates poor self-esteem and social problems Fosters selfishness and survival mentality	Rigid parenting Overstructured, no freedom Creates poor self-esteem with over-reliance on community Fosters extreme self-destruction

Figure 5.1. Four distinct parenting styles.

We want to find the balance of valuing ourselves *and* others. Sometimes those raised in one quadrant try to move out of it, but move to the wrong place. Some from dysfunctional families try to grab for self-esteem, but if they don't learn to value others as well, they may just find chaos. Others from dysfunctional families seek order and move to a more rigid place. This may create some security, but it may further damage their self-esteem. Sometimes those from rigid homes rebel and try to jump to a free style of living (and parenting). But they may toss out some healthy structural principles on the way. The trick is to keep our esteem for others while learning to love ourselves.

Twisted Piety

Another common villain is twisted piety. You hear examples of this from those who grew up in strict religious homes. Pride was a sin. Any inkling of self-satisfaction was roundly discouraged. The message came through loud and clear: We human beings—and you in particular as an ignorant child—are worthless.

This holds true in various religious traditions. I have heard similar stories from Catholics and fundamentalists and others whose parents just wanted them to be good citizens. For some, God is a nit-picking judge who always finds something wrong with your behavior. For others, merely to be human is a sin—we are worms. For still others, it's just bad form to express any good feeling about yourself—good people work well and quietly and fit into the pack. (I think this is a kind of "civil religion" forged in the Depression and fortified in the Fifties—but I'll save that theory for a different book.)

In any case, self-esteem has been damaged by parents or teachers or church leaders who have believed that piety requires self-denigration. Most of these people are devout believers. They have truly tried to do what's right, but they've had a wrong idea about human value.

I don't say this lightly. I realize that many of my readers may fit into this category. This kind of self-denigration is strong in my own evangelical background. In my personal beliefs, I acknowledge the sinfulness of humanity and the need for undeserved grace from God. Pride *is* a sin when a person puts himself above all others and ignores his need for God. But we must find a balance. Religious people of all stripes need to affirm that God made a "very good" humanity, and that he loves us enough to offer us forgiveness for our wrongdoings. (There's more on this subject in chapter 7.)

Twisted Thinking

Our own twisted thinking is sometimes the villain We can many times be our own worst enemies, and we have no one else to blame but ourselves. I believe that we are born with a natural tendency to put ourselves down. I have observed this phenomenon over and over. Children can have wonderful, loving, affirming parents, but they still find ways to deprecate their own worth.

Suppose you were to give a speech before a group, and you had ten people come up to you afterward and tell you how good you were. But then suppose one came up to tell you how you completely missed the point and that you weren't very interesting. Which comment would you remember as you drove home? I know I'm only going to be thinking about that one who didn't like me.

Since I have found this to be almost universally true, I have to conclude that we can't blame it all on our parents or others who put us down. No, I believe that sometimes we just do it to ourselves. In fact I believe this same phenomenon is also in place when we think about how our parents messed us up. They may have told us many good things about ourselves, but when we think about our own childhood, what do we remember? We probably tend to remember only those things that hurt us while growing up.

Cognitive Traps

I call these tendencies "cognitive traps" because they are thoughts we have about our lives and ourselves that lead us into "no win" situations. We can't give ourselves a break, so we are trapped in a negative cycle of self-deprecation.

There are probably hundreds of cognitive traps, but these are some of the most common.

Focusing on the Negative. We discount all of the positive comments people make and instead focus on the one or two negatives. If we do a good job, we consider ourselves lucky, or that it really doesn't count. But when we mess up, then it proves that we really are flawed, or stupid, or that we don't measure up.

Black and White Thinking. In this trap, we either do a job perfectly or it's totally messed up. For example, if the whole house is clean, but one room is a mess, then the house is a mess, or I'm a terrible housekeeper. If I make a wonderful meal, but the rolls are burned, then the meal is ruined.

Magnification of the Problem. We have a way of making mountains out of molehills. We exaggerate our weaknesses and discount our strengths. People who struggle in this area will use "never" and "always" to exaggerate a problem. "You *never* help me." "I'm *always* the one who gets it in the end."

"Should" Statements. These are no-win situations. We can live our whole lives by "shoulds" and find that we never seem to measure up. The truth is we need to be comfortable with just getting by sometimes, because sometimes that's the best we can do.

Accepting Too Much Responsibility. We hold ourselves personally responsible for other people's decisions, even when they are completely out of our control; our children's behavior, our spouse's failures, our co-workers' mistakes.

Catastrophic Events

Throughout our lives, such crises can create many self-esteem problems.

Loss. *Divorce* is one of the most common. For a child whose parents divorce, there are myriad worries.

"Do they both still love me?"

"Did I do something to make Daddy go away?"

"Why couldn't I keep them together?"

"Are my parents bad people? And if so, what does that make me?"

Of course, for an adult struggling with poor self-esteem, a divorce can be disastrous. In my work at Fresh

Start Seminars with those recovering from divorce, I have seen hundreds of people whose sense of self is shattered because they have been rejected by their spouse. And even when they have done the rejecting, there is often a self-loathing that results ("How could I have been so cruel? Am I incapable of having a good relationship?").

Other catastrophic events might include *the death of a parent* (or, later, a spouse); *a serious injury* (especially if it causes an ongoing disability); *a major failure* (Johnny strikes out with the bases loaded, or Jill forgets her lines in the class play); or even *a family move* (it's never easy becoming a "new kid in town").

Aging. Another "catastrophe" that we all face is the aging process. No matter how great our health or looks were in the past, we all succumb to the ravages of time. Even the football star and homecoming queen eventually face this great equalizer. Many adults go through tremendous pangs of insecurity and even depression over their graying (or lost) hair, wrinkles, weight, vision, hearing, and declining health.

Such crises can shake people's faith in everything around them, even their faith in themselves. If there are already self-esteem problems, these crises will usually make them worse.

We are fragile people, many of us. We are Humpty Dumpties, fallen, shattered, waiting to be put "back together again." The healing can happen, but it helps to know what made us fall in the first place.

VOICES

Our informal survey found no lack of villains in people's lives. The variety is fascinating, and the comments are often troubling. Yet many of these people, like you, are working through their troubles and fighting to regain a healthy self-esteem.

We asked them who or what had damaged their self-esteem. Listen to their replies.

"I was cut from the football squad. Dad called me a loser for not making it. I decided to prove him right."

"Teenage peer pressure did some damage. Others seemed more athletic, better looking, more talented, etc."

"I am not usually insecure, except in loving relationships, because of my father leaving my mother when I was a child."

"Both of my parents are perfectionists. My mother was an art teacher and therefore everything has to look perfect. My father always had excellent grades and therefore expected the same of us."

"The institution of the church has been and at times continues to be a damaging and shaming experience, with its 'shoulds' and 'oughts.'"

"My workaholic dad was rarely at home, and my mom was insecure and emotionally unstable. I was not overtly abused in my childhood, but there were many holes."

"My overachieving grandparents set a pace for me to keep. My mother's poor self-image has always frightened me, since I identify with her. Being chubby and an athletic failure as a child led to peer rejection."

"When I was 15, I lost my spot on the wrestling team to a younger kid. That loss made me feel worthless."

"I had one of my gal friends ask a cheerleader (whom I liked) if she would ever like me or go out with me. My friend reported back: 'Patty says she thinks you're cute and everything, but she said you're too short.' That made me feel about two inches tall!"

"My twelve-year marriage was lonely and unfulfilling. The lack of intimacy and warmth from my husband made me feel like I was undeserving."

"My mom was judgmental and critical. But I did a lot of damage to myself. I have been my own worst critic, unable to accept myself."

"I was ridiculed when I was a child, primarily because I was the youngest. No amount of praise from my family would compensate for the teasing."

CHAPTER 6

Confronting the Villains

Speak . . . the truth in love.
—EPHESIANS 4:15 NKJV

In the last chapter, we considered various villains affecting your self-esteem. Recognizing these is an important step. But it's just one of many steps to come. What are you going to do about these villains?

Renounce the Power of the Past

Some counselors recommend that you seek out all those who have done you wrong in the past and confront them with the damage they have caused. I don't. *In some cases,* this may be therapeutic, and I'll discuss that later. But such confrontations can also be fruitless, and sometimes they do more harm than good.

I know a woman who was orphaned at an early age and adopted by a second cousin. All her life, she has struggled with low self-esteem. Through counseling, she has identified her adoptive mother as a "villain" who robbed her of a healthy sense of self. She loves this mother greatly, but she recognizes that the mother did many things to chip away at her, causing major emotional problems later in life.

This woman is now in her forties, the mother in her seventies. I spoke with her shortly after a visit with her mother, and I asked whether they had talked about some of her emotional problems. Had she confronted her mother with the harm she had done?

"No," she said, "I don't know what good it would do now. All my life I have felt that my mother did me a great favor by adopting me and raising me. In return, I have tried to make her happy. At this point, it would only cause her pain if I were to bring up these issues. I need to deal with these things on my own.

"I know that my mother was dealing with her own problems while she was raising me, and I think she probably meant well. I can forgive her for what she has done, whether she knows it or not, and move on with my own life."

Some would say that this is denial, that this strategy merely continues a family dysfunction. But I'm inclined to agree with my friend. It might be different if she wanted (or needed) a deeper relationship with her mother. But by now she has put distance (geographical and emotional) between herself and her mother, and both seem to recognize the limits of their relationship.

But she must—and you must—take unilateral action to renounce the power of the past. After identifying the villains in your personal history, you need to *decide* to break free from their grasp.

If it was some misunderstanding, then remind yourself of the proper understanding of that past event. Remember the precise words that were spoken, and try to interpret them in a more positive way.

If competition with other kids was the culprit, then acknowledge the dog-eat-dog nature of that world, and reinterpret the comments of the past in that light.

If people were just plain mean to you, saying or doing spiteful things, wash your hands of it. That's their problem. If they were hateful toward you, there's nothing you can do about it. Don't get drawn into the maelstrom of hate with them.

I think of the words of Jesus as he hung dying on the cross: "Father, forgive them, *for they do not know what they do*." He was treated as viciously as anyone could be, yet he understood the weakness of his tormentors. They were acting ignorantly. He offered forgiveness freely, whether they wanted it or not.

And that must be our strategy in dealing with the villains of our past. Accept the fact that people do wrong—and for no good reason. If they treated you like a second-class person, it was not because you *were* a second-class person, but because they didn't know what they were doing. *They* were ignorant. *They* were wrong.

Try to find it within yourself to forgive them. I'm not talking about some gushy feeling of forgiveness. I'm talking about cutting the cord, the cord that has stretched through the years, through the decades, connecting you to those past events. As long as you feel spiteful or vengeful about wrongs that were done to you, you are tied to those wrongs, like a dog straining on a leash. And that cord will keep you from moving forward.

I know a man who is haunted by the fact that his high school classmates considered him "least likely to succeed."

Well, he has succeeded. He owns several businesses and is rather wealthy. On a regular basis, he hops into his flashiest car and drives through his hometown, showing off his success to anyone who cares. While I applaud the determination he showed in achieving his success, despite the naysayers, I think he is failing to cut the cords. As long as he has this sense of spite, this overwhelming desire to prove his value to his old classmates, he will not be able to move forward into self-acceptance. He is still fighting the old battles. He needs to let them rest. He needs to say, "I forgive them. They didn't know what they were doing."

But what if it's your own failing that's the villain? *You* struck out. *You* forgot the lines. *You* made a fool of yourself, and you've never been able to forgive that. Well, the same idea applies. You need to acknowledge your own weakness. No one is perfect—that includes you. You have made mistakes, like everyone else. But you can put that behind you now.

In his fine book *Forgive and Forget,* Lewis Smedes summarizes the Dostoevsky novel *Crime and Punishment.* The crime is the murder of an innocent woman, committed by Raskolnikov. The punishment is not only a term in Siberia, but also the self-torture of his own soul.

"Raskolnikov could not forgive himself," Smedes writes. "He tried to excuse himself instead. . . . He was *destined* to kill the old woman. Besides, when you come right down to it, was his act really *that* bad? . . . In clever ways like this he excused himself by finding deep reasons why he was not to blame."

The problem, Smedes says, is that "Raskolnikov did not *dare to be guilty.*"

But in the novel, the murderer does finally accept his blame, specifically and awfully. And then he is able to forgive himself. And thus he is able to love others.

"Release!" Smedes writes. "Release by a discovery that his terrible past was irrelevant to who he was now and was going to be in the future. He was free from his own judgment and this was why he was free to love."

If you are your own villain, you must come face to face with your misdeeds and then have the courage to turn away from them, to forgive yourself, to renounce the power of your past, to cut those cords of guilt.

But *how* do you cut those cords? How do you "renounce the past"? Here are some ideas that may help.

Write Your Own Declaration of Independence

There is something permanent about writing. When you declare something on paper, it's there for you to see—and it remains there. It was one thing for America's founding fathers to take a voice-vote on independence, but quite another to put their "John Hancocks" on the document. So write down those tyrannical memories that have kept your self-image bound, and declare yourself free from them in writing. Announce your forgiveness of those who have troubled you, and explain your intent to put it all behind you. Write yourself a letter and post it where you'll see it (as long as you need to).

Violate the Terms of Your Past Contract

Whether you know it or not, your "villains" succeeded in setting terms for your servitude. You tacitly agreed to put yourself down as often as possible, or to refrain from doing certain adventurous things, or to refuse to act confidently. But part of renouncing the power of the past is breaking that contract. Try something new. Do something you would never have allowed yourself to do before. For my friend with the "bad ankles," it would be to learn how to skate. For you it might be something as simple as complimenting yourself in front of others or volunteering for some new activity.

Stand Guard Against Pesky Memories

You will always need to be vigilant. Be aware when those old messages creep back into your mind. They are from the old regime, but you have renounced its power over you. I would suggest doing or saying something specific when you sense those old messages coming back. Maybe you'll say, "Gone, gone, gone," or "I'm worth more than that," or maybe you'd physically pretend to scoop those thoughts out of your mind and throw them away. Establish a personal ritual that will help you discipline your mind against these thoughts. Obviously there's no hocus-pocus in the words you choose for this ritual or the actions you do, but they can help you banish those self-defeating thoughts more effectively. As you remain watchful against the old messages, they will lose their power over you.

Rebuild Your Personal Story

It is one thing to identify the lies of the past. It is quite another to tell yourself the truth about yourself. But that is the next step. Once you have demolished the false sense of self that the "villains" of your past erected within you, you must start building a new sense of self.

Recovering victims of child abuse learn this. The messages of the past are full of judgment: "I am a bad child; I deserve this treatment; I am not worth love or respect." Once we have renounced those past messages, once we recognize that the fault is not in the child being abused, but in the abuser, the next step is to restore one's own identity. The person must learn to say, "I was not a bad child, I was a victim of a bad person. What's more, I'm a *survivor* of a terrible situation. I have come through quite a lot, with God's help, and I can face difficult circumstances in the future, if need be."

I don't mean to minimize the deep wounds of child abuse. This last paragraph makes recovery sound easy, and it's not. But in any sort of recovery, *cognitive restructuring* is crucial. This applies especially to self-esteem issues. We need to gain a whole new sense of who we are. Most of this restructuring requires us to examine the messages we receive each day, from within ourselves and from the external world. (Later chapters will deal more fully with this.) But some of it requires a reprocessing of our past, a reconstruction of where we have come from.

When I was growing up, I had trouble in school. They put me in the lowest reading group, and I even did poorly there. My classmates considered me dumb, and even my teachers treated me, to some extent, as if I was lacking mental skills. What's worse, I began to think of myself as a "dummy."

Later, my grades improved. My parents considered me a "late bloomer." In high school, I was doing fine academically. I went on to college and graduate school and earned my degrees.

But I still can't spell.

Somehow, when everyone else was learning the basics of spelling in second and third and fourth grades, I was lagging behind. And in that one area, I have never caught up.

This *could* be a matter of great insecurity for me. Imagine a scenario like this:

My secretary comes in with a question about a note I've written. "Reckonsilliation—what's that?"

Now, I could view that as an attack on my intelligence. I could tap into my ancient pains of being a slow learner. From that pain, I could lash out in anger, "Well, if you can't figure it out, maybe I need another secretary who can!"

But that's not the way it goes. I have learned to accept that spelling is something I can't do, and there is no shame in that. I have accepted my past, including those slow-learning years, and I have made peace with that. I know my own limitations, spelling-wise, and I thank God for my secretary and my co-writer and my editors—and the spell-check program on my computer. Essentially, I have "renounced the power of my past." That is, I will not let my poor spelling history affect my attitudes today.

But recently I had a moment of discovery that gave me even more help in processing my past. I was talking with someone about a child's learning disability, and I suddenly realized that was me! I wasn't just a "late bloomer," I must have had a mild learning disability. There is so much that educators know today about the learning process that wasn't known when I was a kid. If they had figured out a way to teach me, to get around those roadblocks in my mind, I would know how to spell today.

This is enabling me to "rebuild my personal story." I

was a victim, of sorts. My mind had funny wiring, and the teachers didn't know enough to jump-start it. But in spite of all that, I pressed on, and learned, and earned my degrees. The negative has turned to positive.

I know that it's not so easy for many people. Your problems may be far worse than just bad spelling. Many suffer the effects of the tragic victimization of child abuse or severe family dysfunction. Others are reaping the results of their own bad choices in the past. The "victim" rhetoric doesn't work as easily when you have victimized yourself.

But the process of rebuilding your personal story involves three major distinctions you must make in order to heal.

Divide What You Have Done from What's Been Done to You

This is the victimization we have been talking about. Users and abusers have a way of making it seem that you're to blame for everything. You're not. See the strength you have displayed in enduring or surviving or confronting these circumstances.

Memories are funny things. Sometimes we "remember" events that never really happened, or we remember things in a distorted way. We package our actual perceptions with a variety of assumptions and conclusions. I find this frequently in counseling couples. The two people remember the same event in entirely different ways. Even the simplest points of fact are up for grabs—not because either one is lying, but because their memories have selectively stored and molded the information. I believe something similar was occurring in the hearings that led to the confirmation of Justice Clarence Thomas. Who was lying—Thomas or Hill? Maybe neither. But both "remembered" the events quite differently.

In remembering an instance of child abuse, someone may say, "I did something very bad, and so my father hit me. I was always doing bad things." But that may not be true at all. It is more likely that the poor child was subject to beatings at the whim of the father, and merely *assumed* that her own misbehavior caused it. In a desperate attempt to make sense of an arbitrary punishment, a child's mind might even manufacture certain misdeeds.

In such cases, it might be helpful to go back and correlate your memories with those of others who knew you back then. I'm not talking now about confronting the "villains," but about comparing notes with other victims or witnesses. One of the most helpful aspects of family therapy is the opening up of closed subjects. As family members discuss mistreatment or dysfunctions in the family, they often feel a sense of vindication: "So it wasn't just me!" Childhood friends or classmates or old teachers or church people or family friends might help you reconstruct your story and get a more objective sense of what you've been through.

In your attempts to distinguish between what you've done and what has been done to you, you may have to admit the feeling that *God* has victimized you. You may feel that you've been created fat or short or ugly—or with a learning disability. Certainly you have done nothing to deserve this, so God must be to blame.

But what many people do—especially religious people—is to reject that notion outright. Blaming God? That's impious, they say, it's sinful. So they conclude (even subconsciously) that they themselves must be at fault after all.

Yet there is a rich religious tradition of wrestling with God over the issues of our lives. Abraham, Jacob, Moses, Job, Paul, and even Jesus were honest enough to argue with God on occasion. There is nothing blasphemous about blaming God for what he has done to us—as long as we move through that into acceptance and, ultimately, a deeper relationship with him. You may someday come to recognize a certain grace in the challenges God has given you, but for now you may just need to realize that you are not to blame.

Divide Who You Are from What You Have Done

Maybe you are to blame for certain aspects of your present situation. You abused drugs, or you betrayed a friend or a spouse, or you wrestle with some life-controlling addiction. But part of rebuilding your personal story means separating yourself from that negative behavior.

You have been saying, "I *am* the bad things I've done. I am worthless. I am incapable of doing anything good." The answer is not to deny that you have done bad things, or even to minimize those things. The answer is to seek forgiveness for the wrong you have done—and to catch a glimpse of that great person God has created you to be.

As a Christian, I see this as the central message of the Bible—the "good news" of the gospel: People do wrong habitually; but God has created people to live brilliantly good lives, and he offers both forgiveness for past misdeeds and spiritual strength for loving deeds in the future.

Divide Who You've Been from Who You Will Be

Every story has a turning point. Scrooge meets his ghosts. Cinderella meets her fairy godmother. Elliott meets E.T.

As you rebuild your personal story, you may need to draw a line in the sand and divide the old from the new. "Yes, I was a ruthless, calculating, no-good jerk. With God's help, I will not be like that anymore." It's easy to get lulled into the assumption that nothing changes, that everything will continue as it has been, "same as it ever was." It's easy to assume that you will continue to be as worthless in the future as you think you've been in the past. But that ain't necessarily so.

Once you have divided your own *actions* from your *victimization,* and your own *being* from your *actions,* if you *still* feel like you're no good—well, tomorrow's a new day. Look to the future with hope. You can write a whole new chapter to your personal story.

(Obviously, the process of changing from a no-good jerk to a decent human being may not be that simple, but it must *start* with a decision to change. That is the point here. Even if you have been a bad person, set your face toward the future and decide to change your ways.)

Reconcile, if Possible, with the Villains

If you have hurt somebody and you want to make amends with that person, it's fairly simple. You go and apologize. You ask the person to forgive you. Then it will be up to that person to decide whether or not to do so.

But if someone else has hurt you, it's more complicated.

Essentially, you need to say, "You have hurt me, and I think you need to apologize." This is not an easy thing. I think many marriages falter on this point as a long-suffering spouse waits and waits for an apology, all the while storing up a grudge.

But if a relationship is to continue, and to grow, the air must be cleared, the wrongs addressed. The hurt parties need to say, "You hurt me," and the villains need to apologize.

It may not be possible to restore a relationship with the people of the past who have hurt you. That's okay. In some cases, it may not be desirable. Here are some instances when you should *not* try to reconcile.

- *When the person is too far away.* You don't need to hire a private detective to hunt down the junior high classmate who teased you. People come and go as we live our lives, and some hurt us and others help us. If your villain is long gone from your life, let it rest. Offer forgiveness unilaterally, and don't let it bug you.
- *When the person is dead.* This goes without saying, right? But some people are deeply troubled by the fact that their parents die before being confronted with the hurts they caused. Reconciliation is thwarted. What makes it worse is that some people idealize the dead, thinking it's in bad form to criticize those who have passed on. In such cases, the hurts remain bottled up, undealt with. The fact is, you can still blame dead villains and you can still forgive them. Obviously, you will never hear their apologies or receive a reconciling hug (not in this world), but you can unilaterally offer forgiveness and let the matter drop.
- *When you're not ready.* You must know who you are before you try to confront your villains. You might storm

into your parents' house and say, "You really messed me up. You made me feel worthless." And they might answer, "There you go again, making us feel bad. You never did care about us." And you're back in the same pit. Remember to rebuild your personal story. That is a crucial step. Unless you have determined where your personal value lies, you will continue to be at the mercy of those villains. An attempted reconciliation could be dangerous.

• *When it would do more harm than good.* This is a tough judgment call (and it's an easy out for those who are scared of this whole business). Earlier in this chapter, I mentioned a woman who decided not to confront her adoptive mother with her "villainy." She decided it was just not worth it. She feared that the mother would not take it well, and that the whole process would be more damaging than healing. I respect a decision like that.

Here are some instances when you *should* attempt a reconciliation.

• *When you have an ongoing relationship.* If you live with or close to the people that have wronged you, you will need to get things straight with them. If your villains are in your family, your church, or your job, and if you have to deal with them regularly, it is probably best to try to clear the air rather than to hide a grudge.

• *When you want an ongoing relationship.* Maybe you have grown distant from family members or former friends who wronged you. Maybe you miss them. The same rule applies: In order for a relationship to grow, there must be openness and honesty, even about these difficult matters.

• *When it is gnawing at you.* If you find that you just

cannot deal unilaterally with this forgiveness issue, then you may need to seek out the person you need to forgive.

• *When you see a threat to someone else.* If you see the same damage being done to someone else—your sibling, a grandchild, other people in the church or at the job—you may need to confront the guilty party.

So how do you go about this reconciling business?

• *Go one to one,* if you are strong enough. If you are not, ask a trusted friend to join you. You are not intending to shame the person publicly, but to address a personal situation. If it is a family situation, you may want to draw the immediate family together for a discussion (especially if the person does not respond to the one-on-one confrontation).

• *Use I-messages.* Don't go in with obvious accusations—"You did this, you did that"—which only gets people's defenses up right away. Instead, say, "I felt this way when you did that." (Someone can deny what he did, but not how you feel.) This carries over into body language as well—do not point.

• *Do not make generalizations.* "You always did this. You never did this." This is probably not true. It is more effective to say, "I often felt this way when you did this."

• *Do not assume motives.* "You were always trying to make life miserable for me" is probably not true. You don't know why the person did what he or she did. Speak of results, not motives.

• *Avoid the old patterns of worthlessness.* You may be walking into a lion's den. Especially if you have been struggling with low self-esteem, this experience could drag you lower. Remember that you are confronting a person who has previously made you feel worthless. It is likely to happen again. Be on guard against those old feelings. As much as possible, take control of the conversation. You are setting new rules now, rules that preserve your self-esteem. Be sure the other person abides by these.

• *Be prepared with self-bolstering self-talk*. You can build a mental fortress for yourself by preparing certain truths to tell yourself when things get rough. "I'm not a little girl anymore." "God has made me a special person." "I am not responsible for that person's happiness." "This is a good thing I am doing now."

• *Speak with grace*. Grace is not eloquence of speech, but a giving spirit. This may mean that you cushion the bad news with a few compliments. "I appreciate the way you always provided for us, but there's this other thing that's been bothering me. . . ." This provides an atmosphere in which the harsher message can be received. Give people the benefit of the doubt. You can leave room for their excuses and still confront them with the pain they caused. It is not your goal to crush them, to destroy *their* self-esteem. It is your goal to deliver a message in a way that they can hear, and perhaps to elicit an apology.

• *Speak the truth*. You *do* have a message to deliver, a message this person needs to hear. Be gracious and loving, but do not shy away from speaking the truth.

What Happens Next?

If the message is received and an apology offered, accept it. Grant forgiveness. Rejoice in your renewed relationship. But also set new boundaries so the relationship does not slip into old patterns.

If the message is not received, hey, at least you've tried. *Do not blame yourself*. "I didn't do a very good job of confronting the person." Of course you didn't! No one does. It's one of the most difficult things anyone has to do. But it's not your fault. It's the other person's fault that you had to do this at all!

But now you have a decision to make. Do you try again, perhaps with support from others? Or do you let the matter drop? It's another judgment call. How important is this relationship to you? How dangerous would another confrontation be to your psyche? What chances are there that the person would listen a second time, or a third time, or a hundredth time?

If you have attempted reconciliation and the person has resisted, do not feel guilty about dropping the issue or even letting the relationship slide. You have delivered the message, like a subpoena, and now the other person knows what's necessary to restore the relationship. Now it's their turn to seek reconciliation.

Sometimes reconciliation with a villain occurs. This is miraculous and wonderful. But often—*often!*—it does not. This is disappointing, but it need not be disastrous. You don't need to recycle all the relationships that have damaged you. You can take out the garbage of past experiences—all by yourself if you need to.

CHAPTER 7

Self-Image and God-Image

Once you're a Catholic, you're always a Catholic in terms of your feelings of guilt and remorse and whether you've sinned or not. Sometimes I am racked with guilt when I needn't be, and that is left over from my Catholic upbringing. Because in Catholicism you're a born sinner and you're a sinner all your life. No matter how you try to get away with it the sin is within you all the time.

—MADONNA, QUOTED IN *THIRD WAY*

Step 5: Discover a Source of Unconditional Love Through a Personal Relationship with God.

Our self-image is frequently a reflection of our image of God and how he views us. While Madonna is neither a role model nor philosopher I would endorse, obviously she has been affected by her religious upbringing. Most would have the impression that she is totally uninhibited, but the quote above indicates otherwise, based on her perception of God.

Three children sat down on a step during their recess period and compared gripes.

"My father's never home," said Wes. "I don't think he cares about me anymore."

"But that means you can do what you want, right?" asked Teresa.

"I guess," Wes answered. "But I almost wish he cared enough to make some rules."

"I don't know," said Teresa. "Some fathers can be pretty strict."

"Tell me about it!" said Calvin.

"Come on," Teresa chided him. "Your dad is great."

"Yeah," Wes agreed. "Your dad really is great. How did you ever deserve a father like that?"

"That's the problem," said Calvin. "He's great, and I stink. He knows everything, and I'm so dumb. I'll never live up to his standards."

"I know the feeling," Teresa muttered.

"Why?" asked Wes. "Is your dad really strict?"

"Yep."

"How do you deal with it?" Calvin wondered.

"I don't," said the girl. "I ran away from home last week."

The three children represent three common religious positions, three distinct views of God and ways of relating to him. In this chapter, we're exploring this thesis: *Your view of yourself is largely affected by your view of God.*

"Calvin": A Worm's-Eye View

As a child in a fundamentalist church, I often sang these beloved words of an Isaac Watts hymn:

Alas, and did my Savior bleed
And did my Sov'reign die?
Would He devote that sacred head
For such a worm as I?

This expresses an important component of fundamentalist theology: We are worms. Compared with God's overwhelming righteousness, we have nothing to offer. Apart from God's grace, we can do nothing good. All our attempts at righteousness are just filthy rags in God's eyes. He is altogether holy, and he cannot bear to look at us in our sinful state. We bear the curse of Adam's sin. We are born sinners, and we live in sin until we encounter God's righteousness in Jesus Christ. Even then, we are pulled down by our basic human tendency to sin. It is a struggle that continues until we are taken to glory.

I'll be straight with you. This is my religious tradition. I grew up believing this, and I still believe it. *But,* it's not the whole story. All the teachings in the previous paragraph come from the Bible. But the Bible has much more to say about human nature.

Try this as the flip side of biblical theology: God made humans as the crowning touch of his creation enterprise. He created man and woman "in his image" and he considered his creation "very good." People sinned, and kept on sinning, but God never stopped loving. Though we had turned away from him, he reached out to us by sending his Son to pay for our sins. By our association with Christ, we are made whole. We are empowered by God's spirit to live righteous lives that please him. We continue to struggle with sin, but Christ gives us victory over it. We can enjoy an "abundant life" here on earth, even as we look forward to an eternity as redeemed humans in God's presence.

Sounds better, eh? And this paragraph is just as biblical as the earlier one.

Ten, fifteen years ago, fundamentalists and evangelicals were railing about the dangers of "humanism." You still hear some of this rhetoric today. Strictly speaking, the foe was *secular* humanism, that is, a belief that places humanity at the pinnacle of existence *and shuts God out of the picture.*

But the matter became muddled so that any positive reference to "humanity" became suspect. It became an either/or situation. Either you exalt God or you exalt humanity—you can't do both. So went the practical assumption, but it was wrong.

Obviously, this view can affect our self-esteem greatly. We *are* human. That is the most basic aspect of our identity. We can't do anything to change that. If our humanity is undesirable—if we are worms—then we're stuck. I once heard a dear Christian woman say, "I want to live righteously, but I'm so *human.*" If I were bolder (or ruder), I would have corrected her. What she meant to say was, "I'm so *sinful,*" or "I *sin so easily.*" Those are things you can work with. You can depend on God's power to sin less, to be more righteous. But if you assume that your humanity prevents you from pleasing God, you're doomed to be in God's doghouse forever.

"I used to see God as the great 'Thou shalt not'—which was due mostly to my earthly father's treatment of me. I've been liberated from that thinking as I've sought to know more of who God really is. It's only through

his love for me that I'm who I am today."
—A respondent to our survey

What's the solution? We need to understand that humanity is not the problem; sin is the problem. Humanity is a beautiful creation of God. He made us to be his friends. Sin is the aberration that keeps us from him—but Christ has conquered sin! We *can* please God as we rely on his Spirit to live righteous lives. We will stumble, but God welcomes us back into his friendship. We need not be sorry for our humanness. On the contrary, we should thank God for it (as humans we are "crowned . . . with glory and honor"—Psalm 8:5 NKJV). We need to be sorry only for our sin. And for that, God offers forgiveness through Christ.

This is not a new theology. It is squarely within the biblical/fundamentalist/evangelical doctrine. But too many of us have only been playing one side of that record.

Steve was a staunchly conservative Christian who came to me suffering from severe guilt feelings. He told me how he hated himself. He just could not keep from sinning, and so he doubted whether he really had a relationship with God. I assured him that we Christians do sin, but that God forgives us. Each Wednesday, when he came in for counseling, Steve would be reassured by my words. He would go home in a good mood. But each Sunday he would hear his preacher describing how true believers should be living, and how ashamed everyone should feel for not living that way. This would sink Steve deep into despair. He would isolate himself from others because he felt he was so bad. Sometimes he would actually go home and bang his head against a wall, trying to punish himself for not living up to God's standards.

Though I would never prescribe that a person go to a certain church, in this case I suggested that Steve look for a church that emphasized the grace of God, rather than judgment. He did, and his situation improved.

Steve felt that he was worthless because of his sin, and this was underscored each Sunday by his preacher. But that is not the overriding message of the Bible. The Bible teaches that, despite our sin, God considers us so desirable that he goes to extraordinary lengths to have a relationship with us. His love is unconditional; it supersedes the worst of our sin. Steve did not have to punish himself. It was God's supreme love that took the punishment on Steve's behalf.

"I tend to see God as punitive, not all-loving or forgiving or accepting."
—A respondent to our survey

"Wes": Absentee Father

Many religious people are functional atheists. They know God is out there somewhere, and that he gave us some guidelines about loving each other, but he's not very involved in our lives. Like "Wes" in our children's story, we can do what we want. There aren't many rules. But there isn't much paternal attention, either. At least not that we can see.

I will admit that I am removed from this situation. My experience is in the evangelical tradition, which tends to hold the "worm's-eye view," as described above. That I know firsthand; this I know only through observation. This makes me hesitate in pointing fingers, but let me say that I see this "absentee father" motif mostly in the liberal Protestant denominations (in some, but certainly not all, churches) and among casual attenders in many denominations. And of course it occurs among many nonreligious folks as well.

If God exists, he is an idea, a principle, some all-pervading force—but not very personal or present with us. Or maybe he's the clockmaker who wound up our world and has dozed off since. In any case, according to this view, it's pretty much up to us to live the best way we know how.

This is precisely the "secular humanism" that so many evangelicals have been decrying. On the surface, you would expect no self-esteem problems. Humanity is exalted. We are the operating sovereigns of our world, right? With no rules, there's no guilt. I'm okay, you're okay, okay? Do whatever you think best, as long as you feel good about it.

"God is my source of identity. Knowing that he has a purpose for my life has made a tremendous difference. No matter how I may be feeling, the reality is that God is constant. He loves me and he does not make any mistakes. What a relief!"
—A respondent to our survey

But there's something shallow in this approach. Cut off from a relationship with a personal God, humanity loses its value. If we are not the creations of a great God, we become just the latest model in a haphazard evolutionary process. And what really is the value of a human being as compared to, say, a dolphin or a seal or a slug? What I feel good about may feel bad to you, so there's chaos.

With no solid standards of behavior, despair sets in. We feel an internal vacuum.

Our self-esteem suffers, and we don't understand why. We should feel good about ourselves, but we just feel lost. It's the absentee-father syndrome, in a spiritual sense. We don't know who we are, because we don't know where we have come from. We wind up looking for love in all the wrong places. We search for that sense of spiritual meaning in our romantic relationships, in our work, in our causes. But the unconditional love that we long for remains out of our grasp.

What's the solution? Recover a sense of a personal God. I know of no other way out of this mess. Open your eyes and see God at work all around you, in your life, in your family. Yes, God is an idea, far bigger than we could ever fathom, but he also presents himself as a person. Seek a relationship with this powerful but caring person. See your own value as the handiwork of this Creator and accept your Creator's all-encompassing love.

"Much of my self-worth comes from the knowledge of God's creating and loving me."
—A respondent to our survey

"Teresa": The Lapsed

Our third child is the runaway, Teresa. She had strict parents and couldn't live up to their standards, so she left.

There are millions of people who have given up on their faith because they just couldn't play by the rules—and they feel terrible about it.

I see many lapsed Catholics who fit this mold. They started missing mass, then skipping confession, they got divorced or use birth control, and they just couldn't keep up with the church anymore. There are also many lapsed fundamentalists and evangelicals, refugees from strict churches that disapproved of their lifestyle or their doubts. And I'm sure there are "runaways" from rigid religious groups in the Eastern Orthodox and Jewish traditions as well.

What these runaways have in common is *background*. Some were brought up in Catholic or fundamentalist schools. Or at least Sunday school taught them about God and his standards. Their knowledge of God is usually just enough to be dangerous: The Ten Commandments, which seem impossible to uphold. The image of God as all-holy Judge. Perhaps the terrible picture of Christ suffering on the cross for *our* sins.

The guilt is overwhelming.

Catholics and fundamentalists catalog sins differently, but both groups have their lists. And many souls have grown weary in maintaining the lists of their own shortcomings. How could God possibly love them, considering all they've done? And so they ditch the faith.

But those cords are not easily severed. The guilt remains buried deep in a person's soul, no matter how much he or she may deny it: God is angry. God judges me. My sin put Christ on the cross.

Self-esteem is thus a difficult thing to come by, since your soul is fundamentally flawed. You can do all the right things to feel good about yourself, but you always have this sense that God is up there and he's not happy with you.

In my work with Fresh Start seminars, I have met with thousands of divorced Christians. Unfortunately, most churches have been slow to care for such people. At the time of their worst spiritual crisis, many of these people feel abandoned by their churches. And so they slip out the back door. For the rest of their lives, they feel branded by their divorce. They feel ostracized by other Christians. And many have just given up going to any church at all. I sense a lot of anger among these people, but also a lot of self-doubt.

I know this because I've been there. After my divorce, I went through several years of strong self-doubt—spiritually and in every other way. I had strayed from the "perfect will of God" and I was doomed to wander. Or so I feared. I felt rejected by God and by the church, and I was angry about that. If God doesn't want me, I thought, then I don't want him either. I was a runaway, cut off from any spiritual nourishment, divorced from my own identity as a valued child of a loving God.

What's the answer? Acquaint yourself with the love of God. That's what I had to do—get a whole new picture of a God who loved me no matter what I did.

Read your Bible again. Or go to a different church that will tell you about forgiveness. Transform your image of God from Judge to Lover. The Bible teaches that God pities us as a loving father has compassion on his kids. God understands our failings and offers forgiveness. When he forgives us, he removes our sins "As far as the east is from the west" (Psalm 103:12 NKJV).

"I think one of the reasons that I struggle is that I believe that I have to earn people's love as well as God's love."
—A respondent to our survey

Recall the story of the prodigal son (Luke 15) and see yourself as that runaway. The loving father rushes with open arms to welcome you back. That is how valuable you are.

You can try to keep ignoring your guilt feelings, but that won't work for long. Or you can deal with the guilt by going to the source. Ask for God's forgiveness *and accept it.* And start a new kind of relationship—not with a meter maid who writes you tickets for each offense, but with a friend who helps you through the struggles of life.

"When I look to my talents and strengths for self-esteem, it is a vicious cycle—it is performance-based. It is only my belief in the dignity of man and our being loved by God that gets me out of it, to where I can enjoy my strengths and work on my weaknesses."
—A respondent to our survey

CHAPTER 8

You Can Beat the System

Do not give dogs what is sacred; do not throw your pearls to pigs. If you do, they may trample them under their feet, and then turn and tear you to pieces.

—MATTHEW 7:6 NIV

Step 6: Decode Society's Sinister Messages and Break Free of Them.

From Madison Avenue to Hollywood and Vine, the system manages to twist our values. But what about Main Street, U.S.A.? How does our self-esteem fare in the activities of everyday life?

Not too well. Wherever you go, the competition is fierce. Go to the gym, and people with perfect bodies and skimpy outfits are sneering at you. Go to a PTA meeting and the other parents are crowing about their darlings' latest accomplishments (and questioning your parental skills). Drive down the street in your Ford Taurus, and your neighbor may pass you in his Mazda RX-7. Even at church, others may subtly judge you for not meeting their standards of clothing, propriety, or Bible knowledge.

If your self-esteem is already shaky, this competition can be devastating. The backstabbing, the snide comments, the preening and posing—these can easily derail your self-confidence. Society is a rat race. And even if you win, you're still a rat.

I often talk about the four B's, the criteria for success according to today's world—Beauty, Brawn, Brains, and Bucks. The indoctrination starts in our childhood. Who are the most popular kids? The strongest and prettiest. The world revolves around those people. They get the dates. They get the acclaim. At some point in high school, the circle enlarges to include the brainy kid who's headed to a prestigious college (and can help you with your homework), and the rich kid who drives the flashy car. In adulthood, brawn is less important, and bucks are crucial.

"The system" is built foursquare on these cornerstones. If you have just one of these things, you crave the other three. If you have none, what good are you? (At least that is what society would teach us.)

This, too, is false. Advertisers promise these qualities, the media display them, and society buys it—but the value of a person does not reside in Beauty, Brawn, Brains, or Bucks. Our personal worth is built on stuff more solid.

There is one other conspirator I should mention—the workplace. As "the system" tries to make you think less of yourself, your workplace may be a major factor in undermining you. Some bosses feel threatened by any show of confidence, so they make it a point to put you down whenever they can. Your work is never quite good enough. It's the carrot-on-a-stick routine. To keep you working hard, they'll withhold the reward for a job well done. They wouldn't want you to get ideas of grandeur—why, that might lead to a promotion or a raise or something. You might even take *their* job. No, they need to keep you hungry.

In some occupations, there is great competition among co-workers. Your office mates may do all they can to exalt themselves at your expense.

For other workers, it's the job itself that gets them. A friend of mine told me that he would never work in sales because the percentage of success is so low. Every time a potential customer said no, he took it as a personal rejection. Others are locked into pointless, go-nowhere routines that whittle away their self-respect day by day. Maybe they're doing things that they really don't do well. Or maybe they just don't see how their work benefits society.

So the workaday world can further erode our self-esteem, another element in "the system" that puts us down. The system is big and powerful and we can't get away from it. With all this talk about "conspiracy," I'm not suggesting that you run off to a cave somewhere or start stockpiling weapons. We live in this world, and we can't avoid its pressures. But there are some things we can do to guard ourselves against the damage of the messages that surround us each day.

Advertising and the Media

Turn Off

The biggest weapon against destructive TV messages is the Off button. It's silly to sit there watching *Baywatch* reruns and feeling guilty that you quit working out ten years ago. *Turn off* the TV and go work out! Okay, you may never look as good as those hunks and babes, but who cares? Don't let their "perfect" looks distract you when you could be doing something productive. I guarantee it—your life will not be impoverished if you turn off that show. Or many other shows. Remember: You have ultimate control of that remote control. You can guard your eyes and ears from self-defeating images and messages.

This is easy to say and hard to do. In our society, TV is a drug. Most of us have made it an integral part of our lives. We adapt our schedules to it, physically and emotionally. Changing our TV habits might be like kicking an addiction. But that's where we need to start.

Examine the value of the shows you watch on TV. Are they enticing you into a fantasy world? How do they affect your view of yourself? Are you less satisfied with your own life after watching certain programs?

Start with just one show that you find especially damaging to your self-esteem. Decide to do something else instead of watching it. Enlist the help of your family or friends.

Once you've kicked the habit of one damaging show, do the same with another. Then extend the process to your selection of videos and movies. Reestablish your control over the entertainment that enters your mind.

No matter how carefully you choose the programs you watch, you are bound to see some of those commercials that tear you down. And you will still see the billboards and flip through magazines with these ads. You will always encounter these messages. You can't get away from them all. The trick is to *recognize* these bad messages and *talk back* to them.

Through the years there has been a lot of talk about subliminal messages in advertising. "Subliminal messages" are certain images that are hidden within the pictures we see, planting a suggestion deep within our minds about the desirability of the product. Whether or not such messages are really there, the erosion of our self-esteem occurs mostly on a subliminal level. We don't even recognize that a toothpaste commercial, say, has made us doubt the beauty of our own smile. Because of a deodorant commercial, many of us are now afraid to raise our arms in public—but it doesn't occur to us as we're watching it that this is a damaging message.

We have become inured to the abuse we get from the media. Slowly, over the years, we have grown used to it. It's like the frog in the kettle. If you want to boil a frog (I don't know why you'd want to, but so goes the story), don't put him in boiling water—he'll hop out. No, heat the water slowly, so the frog doesn't even know what's happening. Thus has it happened with the ads we see. We don't even know what's happening.

So look for those messages. Be aware of what ads are saying about who you are. That's the first line of defense.

Talk Back

The next is to talk back to the TV or magazine or billboard. Say it out loud: "That's not true!" The people around you may think you're crazy but, hey, why not get them into the game too?

Did you ever play the "I spy" game as a kid? Well, this is a new game, "I spy the lie." (It's actually not a bad idea for a family to play this during an evening in front of the TV.) When you see an advertisement that's implying or stating something that's not true, say so! "I *don't* need that car. I'm perfectly happy with the one I have."

By exposing these messages for what they are, we are fighting the system. We are defusing the time bombs planted in our heads. We are recognizing the subliminal communication and rejecting it.

Try the Positive

Then we can put our money where our mouths are. Instead of just badmouthing the ads that put us down, we can reward the companies that present good messages—we can *try the positive*. I don't know that we'll make a big impact on the advertising industry, but every little bit helps.

Around every major election, people decry the high negativity of the campaign. Every candidate, it seems, tries to smear his or her opponents. Mudslinging is rampant. Voters are forced to choose the lesser of two (or more) evils. Newspaper editorials bemoan this terrible state. People groan, "Why can't the candidates just talk about the positive aspects of their own records?"

For one very good reason. Mudslinging works. Yes, the voters hate it. Yes, it besmirches the whole campaign, the whole system. But if you are behind in the polls, the quickest way to gain ground is to uncover (or manufacture) some scandal involving your opponent. And if mud has been slung at you, you will be discredited unless you sling some mud in return.

The point is this: We can complain all we want about negative messages, but nothing will change until we start rewarding the positive messages with our votes and our purchases. Candidates don't care what we say, they care only about which lever we pull. Advertisers don't care whether or not we like their ads—only whether or not their ads make us buy things.

Fear is a great motivator. Insecurity is even better. Advertisers keep making us doubt ourselves for one very simple reason—it works. If we, through careful attention and courageous response, can immunize ourselves to these damaging messages, maybe we can make a difference.

The Job

We tend to define ourselves by what we do. Ask ten people who they are, and eight will tell you their occupation.

"I'm a lawyer."

"I'm an editor."

"I'm in retailing."

This has always been true of men, but increasingly women do it too. You are your job.

That makes it all the more devastating when your job is dragging you down. If you are what you do, and you are feeling incapable of doing what you do, then who are you, anyway? How can you survive when the very core of your self-understanding is threatened?

Three words: Diversify, integrate, and shield.

Diversify

You need to redefine yourself. You need to expand your self-understanding. Stop seeing yourself as just a "lawyer," just an "editor." Get a bigger picture of who you are and what you do.

Throw Yourself into Relationships. Besides being "in retailing," chances are you're also a husband or wife, boyfriend or girlfriend, mother or father, daughter or son, and surely you are a friend. Try defining yourself, in part, by these relationships. This may mean investing more time and effort in these relationships. But it's worth it.

"I may be an average executive or a so-so secretary," you'll be able to say, "but I'm a great friend. My boss may think I'm worthless, but my family would disagree." Those relationships will anchor your self-understanding.

Develop a Hobby or Sideline. Take up singing or sailing, baseball cards or Barbie dolls. Write that novel you've been kicking around in your head or learn to paint. Get a real estate license or run for the school board. Start your own business in your home or try out for a community play. There are hundreds of ways to invest your spare time that can bring you great satisfaction. That will lessen the effect of a bad experience at work, if you can get the needed strokes from your extracurricular pursuits.

Get Involved in a Good Cause. Many people get involved in church ministries. They'll work their 35 hours a week, but what's really important is their service for God. Maybe you can tutor kids in the inner city and make a huge difference in their lives. Maybe you can publicize the needs of hungry people in other countries or the homeless in America. Maybe you can visit people in the hospital or in prison.

One of the most basic human needs, emotionally, is the need for significance. We need to make a difference somehow, somewhere. Some people have jobs that meet this need, but many don't. Yet if you diversify your own efforts—finding significance in relationships, hobbies, or good causes—you can meet that basic need.

Integrate

Donna got a job as a receptionist in a doctor's office. At first she was concerned about all there was to learn in this new job, but she mastered it pretty easily. Then it got boring. She complained to me about how meaningless it all was. Would she be stuck there forever?

The next time I saw her, it was as if someone had turned on a light. I asked about her job and she spoke very differently about it—her whole attitude had changed.

"I realized," Donna said, "that these people coming into the doctor's office are full of pain and worry. I have to give them forms to fill out, but I can also give them some love. If they see a friendly face and hear a kind word, maybe it will help them feel better. They're very needy when they come in there, and maybe I can make a difference."

There's that "significance" thing. Donna was able to integrate her core self with her job in a meaningful way. She found a way to express herself, and to find personal worth, in the routine of her job.

That isn't always easy. But it is possible in most jobs where you deal with people. Can you touch your customers' lives in meaningful ways? Not huge ways, necessarily. But can you smile, and care, and get a step beyond the token "Have a nice day"?

What about your co-workers? Can you make a difference in their lives by being a good listener, a resource, a comforter, an encourager? You may be putting nuts on bolts in an assembly line, but you can still help to create a joy-filled environment.

Try to redeem your daily work by integrating, as much as you can, your core values with the job.

Shield

Sometimes a boss or co-worker makes the job miserable. There's not a whole lot you can do.

As a teenager I worked flipping burgers at a fast-food joint. One of the other burger-flippers, John, older and more experienced, decided to make life difficult for me (and for every other rookie). He regularly berated us for every little mistake, and he often invented "mistakes" to yell at us about. We were ignorant, unskilled losers as far as John was concerned, and he never let us forget it.

It got to me. Night after night of his needling—I couldn't take it. After all of five weeks, I quit. Looking back on it now, I realize that I was probably a pretty decent burger-flipper. It was John who had the problem. He was probably the classic case of the guy who hates himself and takes it out on everyone else. He hated what he was doing and was probably jealous of anyone who seemed to be headed toward a better future—and that included me. You find people like John wherever you go.

Maybe it would have been different if I knew how to shield myself from John's attacks. Shielding is mostly a matter of self-talk. You redefine the situation within your own mind in a way that allows you to continue working with minimal emotional damage.

I'm Okay, You're Not. The first tactic is merely a matter of placing the blame for the situation squarely on the other person. This could have been my tactic with John, who obviously was unhappy with everything. If I had been able to place the blame back on him, then I could have felt better about my own work. With this tactic, you're saying: "This person has a problem. I will do what I have to do in order to survive in this situation, and I may have to bend over backwards to please this person, but I can do that. It's not my problem. It's the other person's problem. And being the nice human being that I am, I'll live with it."

Understand: You may still have to work harder or endure unfair conditions, but at least you are not personalizing the situation. It's not your problem. You are not letting this person do a number on your self-esteem. You are shielding yourself from the emotional attack.

Whatever You Say, Boss. In some cases, it's not that your boss has emotional problems that are turned toward you, but he or she may just have different values. Often, bosses are totally dedicated to their jobs and to the company and expect everyone else to be as gung-ho as they are. If you're not, they put you down. Or they may be sold on a certain direction for the company that you don't agree with. They may even require that you lie or cheat on their behalf, which may require a tough moral decision on your part (and perhaps a search for a new job). If you don't comply, they question your value to the company (or your value to anyone).

In such cases, this second shielding response goes something like: "As a good employee, I will work as well and as diligently as I can. But I have limits. These limits are part of who I am, and I can be proud of them. You have no right to demean me for standing by my limits. You are hiring me to do my work, but you can't buy my soul."

Shut Down. When things get so bad that you can't deal with a boss or co-worker, you may need to "shut down" your emotional response to them. If they insist on tearing down your self-image, you may need to shield yourself by not even hearing what they say. If they give you necessary instructions for a task, fine. But if they start berating you, just let it go in one ear and out the other.

Obviously, these are worst-case scenarios. If it gets this bad, you may need to quit. But if you can't, if you need to keep the job, some degree of shielding may be necessary. In these cases, the integration of your core values with your work could be very important. You may, for instance, need the support of your co-workers to deal with a destructive boss. You should also diversify so that there's some source of self-worth your vicious boss cannot touch.

Society

The people around us seem to worship in the false pantheon of Beauty, Brawn, Brains, and Bucks. Let me suggest that we pointedly replace those things with the virtues of Caring, Diligence, Humor, and Loyalty.

Beauty—or Caring?

"Physical beauty is only skin deep," we say, but few of us live that way. We strive to make ourselves more beautiful on the outside, and we flock around those who possess external beauty.

Can we replace beauty with *caring*? That is the mark of a beautiful spirit. The person who truly loves others—who gives of himself or herself to help others—this is the one we should applaud and seek to emulate. We need to cultivate that caring spirit as carefully as we primp in front of the mirror.

Evaluate your own habits:

• How much time do you spend each day trying to look better? Compare that to the time you spend caring for other people. If this is out of balance, make a point to change it. You may need to spend less time in front of the mirror. You may need to seek out ways to help others.

• Are there friends or acquaintances that you envy because of their physical beauty? Try to control this by focusing more on the inner spirit. When you see these people, tell yourself, "I am beautiful inwardly, and that's more important."

• Do you choose friends on the basis of physical appearance? Or do you treat your good-looking friends better than your ordinary-looking friends? If so, stop it. This doesn't mean you need to dump your attractive friends, but try to move all your friendships to a deeper, inner-spirit level.

Brawn—or Diligence?

Brawn—physical strength—is prized in our competitive, sports-oriented world. But can we replace it with *diligence* as our desired virtue? Diligence is the ability to work hard, the willingness to use one's strength to do good things.

The sports world is full of strong, physically talented people. But there's something special about the person who may lack the innate skills and yet works hard to win a place on the team. Fran Tarkenton was a pipsqueak of a quarterback who sometimes found it hard to see over his huge offensive line. But he developed his passing and scrambling skills to become one of the best quarterbacks the NFL has ever seen. In the Philadelphia area, our ice hockey legend is Bobby Clarke. While he's not the fastest skater or the sharpest shooter, his sheer tenacity led his team to the Stanley Cup and earned him a Most Valuable Player award.

Obviously we need to reach outside the sports world for the full application of this truth. Why worship the sports heroes when you are exercising diligence in your family life or at your job or in your church? As you apply yourself to a task—whether it's helping Junior with his homework or meeting a major deadline at work—aren't you showing a quality far more important than any grand slam or slam dunk requires?

We need to get our priorities straight. I'm not saying you can't root for your favorite team. But don't worship them. Don't envy them. Learn to root for yourself, too, as you go through the adventure of your own life.

Brains—or Humor?

Brains, now there's a quality to worship, right? Intelligence is something we desperately need, and those who have it are a cut above, right?

Not necessarily. Like beauty and brawn, intelligence is a gift. A person can do a few things to develop it, but it's still a gift. No person can say, "I have become intelligent by my own doing!" God dispenses this gift in different degrees. All that matters is what you do with what you've got.

Let me throw you a curve now by suggesting that we replace our worship of intelligence with an appreciation for *humor*. Humor, too, is a kind of knowing. It's knowing your limits. A person with a good sense of humor knows he is not perfect, accepts that fact, and can laugh about it. Even the most intelligent person needs to know what she does not know, and accept it and somehow work with it. You will never know everything, so you might as well have some fun.

A friend of mine is involved in a new church. This church started from scratch a few years ago, and it has seen phenomenal growth. It has made a point of *not* stealing members from other churches, and instead it has focused on the most difficult audience: those who have not been involved in a church. Still, it has attracted nearly four hundred people in less than three years.

How has this happened? To what do they attribute their success? Great preaching? "Well," my friend says, "the preaching's quite good, but I don't think that's it." Brilliant planning? "Definitely not. We had some good ideas, but we seldom executed them well."

Then what is it?

"On a human level," my friend says, "the most attractive element of our church is our sense of humor. We just don't take ourselves that seriously. We have become very aware of our own limitations in starting this church. We have made big plans, and we have often botched them, but God has had a better idea. He has made things happen in spite of us. That has resulted in a deep sense of humility, of faith, and of humor. I think the congregation has caught that."

You will never know as much as you'd like to know. There will always be someone else whose brilliance puts you to shame—if you allow yourself to be shamed by that. But there is great grace in humor, knowing what you don't know, and accepting that.

Bucks—or Loyalty?

Our world is run by those who have the bucks. "Money makes the world go 'round." In a way, this is the most absurd of all these false gods we've been discussing.

I just spoke with Jim, a single man whose girlfriend left him for someone with more money. As you might expect, he is devastated. But the devastation is taking a strange direction. It's not just the pain of losing her or the disappointment of what she turned out to be—this man is severely doubting his own value. "If only I could provide for her better," Jim moaned. "But I don't have anything to offer her, and he does."

This is patently untrue, as I pointed out to him. Jim is a caring soul who has gone into a helping profession rather than a more lucrative career. He works hard, he has a great sense of humor, and he's fiercely loyal. He had plenty to offer this woman, probably far more than her new beau has—but her values were screwed up.

While I worked in the Philadelphia school system, I had a teacher tell me that she could never date a man who did what I did. Why? She said she could never respect a man who settled for so little money. If I had been insecure, her words would have cut me deeply and might have kept me from dating for a while. But instead I remember feeling sorry for her. "You mean it's okay for you to teach here," I asked, "but you don't respect me for being a counselor here?"

"That's right," she replied. "I don't need money because I'm going to marry a man who is ambitious and successful." And I wondered what kind of self-image would come up with a goal like that.

Two years later, she did marry. A lawyer, in fact.

I ran into her recently. She was coming to our counseling center for help. She was depressed, totally unhappy with her life. Her husband is constantly working, and she feels like she has nothing worthwhile to offer.

How absurd it is to think that money makes someone a better person! And yet that is exactly what this teacher thought. That's what Jim was fearing in his fit of self-doubt—"If only I had more money, I would be worth more to her." To *her,* maybe—in her twisted thinking—but not in any larger sense. Beauty, brawn, and brains are all at least connected to a person in some way. They are not as important as everyone thinks, but at least they're part of who you are. But money, that's not even *you*. It's something you have. How could that possibly make you a better person? Yet millions of "have-nots" look up to the "haves" and envy them: "If only I had what they have. . . ."

Every so often you'll read the story of a lottery winner whose life was changed dramatically by the influx of money. And not changed for the better. They move to a ritzier neighborhood where they don't know anyone. They become suspicious of their friends and relatives. They quit their jobs. They focus on buying the pleasures of life. In the process, they cut off all their social connections. They isolate themselves. In short, they move from people to things. And their lives stink.

Money cannot buy happiness. And it certainly cannot buy personal value. You are worth much more than your bank account.

Let me suggest that we replace our devotion to bucks with a devotion to *loyalty*. Money is just something you have; loyalty is what you do with what you have. How do you invest yourself? Can your friends, neighbors, and coworkers count on you to be honest, to give of yourself, to pitch in when they need help? I don't mean pitch in with money. I mean that you offer whatever you have—time, attention, concern, prayers, humor, support, a place to stay.

Money is fickle. A person with money will tend to go wherever there's the best deal. But a person with loyalty will sink roots deep into a relationship, a cause, a neighborhood.

Beauty, brawn, brains, and bucks are things that are given to some people. They are not fair measures of a person's value. If you don't have these things, there's not a whole lot you can do to get them.

But caring is something you can apply yourself to. You can develop your inner spirit and establish habits of reaching out to others. You can gain inner beauty.

Diligence is something you can choose to use. Whatever your physical strength, you can achieve great things through hard work.

Humor is a letting go, an accepting. You don't need to be the life of the party, you just need to accept your limits and be willing to enjoy them. This, too, is something you can develop.

Loyalty is an investment—but a less material kind. Whether or not you ever earn big bucks, how do you invest all those wonderful qualities you have?

Our society is a rat race, as I've said. People are scrambling to get ahead in one area or another. But pause a moment to consider what the rat race would be like if no one hurried. What if no one really cared about being first?

What if we had such caring and loyalty that we gave each other the right of way?

I read once about a race in which the leader was nearing the finish line, but looked back and saw that another contestant had stumbled. He went back to help him up, and they crossed the finish line together.

It happened in the Special Olympics, for children with disabilities. There the emphasis is not on finishing first, but just finishing. In that context, the story makes a lot of sense. But what a picture it is of how life could be for all of us! If we could just discard our "me-first" values of beauty, brawn, brains, and bucks, and develop some deeper virtues of caring, diligence, humor, and loyalty, maybe we could all reach the finish line with wholeness and self-respect.

"The system" can be brutal. But we can fight back. With careful monitoring and courageous response, we can defuse the bombs that would blow up our self-esteem, and we can even help others maintain theirs.

CHAPTER 9

Exercising Your Gifts

Opportunity is missed by most people because it is dressed in overalls and looks like work.

—THOMAS EDISON

One of my favorite stories in the Bible is the story of Joseph. His jealous brothers sold him into slavery, but he rose to a prominent position in the house of a very rich man in Egypt—only to be thrown into prison when he was falsely accused by the rich man's wife.

Joseph then spent several years in prison and gained a reputation among the other prisoners as a man of great wisdom. Even though everything had gone wrong for Joseph, and outwardly he looked like a complete failure, he still led with his strengths and was able to help others in that dungeon.

But then something even more remarkable happened. Pharaoh sent for Joseph! Pharaoh was the ruler of the greatest power on earth at that time. And yet we can't begin to compare him to our President, because this man had absolute power. We know that when someone displeased him, he would have him beheaded or thrown into prison until he felt like letting him out. I'm sure that Joseph, being a prisoner, was very aware of this.

Pharaoh had dreamed a dream. He had just fired all of his wise men because none of them could interpret his dream. But one of Pharaoh's servants (who had served some time in prison) recommended Joseph as a dream-reader. So the mighty Pharaoh summoned the prisoner Joseph.

The Bible then says that the guards had Joseph cleaned up, and gave him some better clothes. I envision a man who looked much worse than a street person. He had been in prison for several years. He was dirty, his clothes were in rags, his hair and beard were a mess, and I'm sure he smelled quite ripe. Yet he was quickly cleaned up and brought before the most powerful man in the whole world. What would your self-image be at that point? What would your inner voice be saying to you then?

Joseph goes on to interpret Pharaoh's dream, and gives the credit to God. This is incredible enough, but the part that amazes me most comes next. According to Joseph, the dream was predicting a seven-year famine. So not only does Joseph interpret the dream, but he proceeds to tell Pharaoh what he should do about the coming famine—how he should run the country! Keep in mind that Pharaoh only asked Joseph to interpret the dream. I'm sure that he never asked Joseph to tell him how to run his empire. Also, Joseph did not have time to rehearse a speech. This was Joseph using his God-given wisdom to use this petrifying experience as an opportunity. God had given Joseph an opportunity and Joseph not only walked through that open door, but he walked through it *boldly!*

I had an experience that seems similar in some respects (though not nearly as dramatic). After going through a divorce, I faced one of the most difficult times of my life. I had little or no self-confidence left, due to the loss of my wife, the loss of many of my friends, the loss of my ministry, and the eventual loss of my home and all of my savings. I worked in a delicatessen for a while and then worked for a year as a night janitor in a school. You can imagine how good I felt about myself as high school boys and girls laughed and made comments about me behind my back. I can assure you that I did not handle myself as well as Joseph. I grew angry and depressed. I was mad at God and thought very little of myself. Forget about any kind of social life. I was convinced that my life would consist of merely existing from day to day, with no joy, no love, and nothing to really live for.

It was actually my best friend who helped me through that difficult time. Just as we've described what it means to become your own best friend, in this situation, my friend continued to pursue me, encourage me, respect me, and pushed me to respect myself. As I grew in confidence and as he encouraged me to rebuild my life, we began to brainstorm. "What do you think you do well? What have you always wanted to do? If you could do whatever you wanted, what would it be? What would it take for you to reach that point?" My friend believed in me and encouraged me when I no longer believed in myself.

Some of my ideas were off the wall. I wanted to join the CIA, and be a covert intelligence agent. The CIA didn't return my calls. I wanted to travel the world and see all the things the world had to offer; but there was no money in it. More realistically, I wanted to help young people. People who were looking for guidance and direction in their lives. "I know! I could be a guidance counselor!"

This led to a two-year guidance counseling program, which opened the door for a school psychology degree, which led to a Ph.D. program, which opened the door for me to become a licensed psychologist, which allowed me to open a counseling center, which grew more quickly than I ever imagined, which gave me the opportunity to hire fourteen other counselors, and which also has given me the chance to speak to people around the country and to write books, which will open doors for new opportunities, which I still cannot begin to imagine. You might say that I've been very lucky. I prefer to believe that God has opened some doors for me, and I'm determined to walk through them *boldly*. I now believe in myself, and I think I have a fairly accurate view of my own strengths and weaknesses (and I'm still learning and evaluating myself).

Step 7: Find Something You Can Do Well and Then Do It.

Through evaluation by yourself, your friends, and perhaps a counselor, you need to determine at least a few things that you do well. If you have a hard time coming up with ideas, try asking yourself the same kinds of questions I asked myself some fourteen years ago:

- What have I always wanted to do?
- What kinds of activities give me pleasure?
- Where can I go to learn more about these skills and activities?

Sometimes the answers to these questions can seem overwhelming. "I could never do that!" "That would take too long." "Do you have any idea how hard that would be?" "I can't do anything well!"

Before you answer all these objections, once again I have to ask you, what would you tell your best friend? If you're like me, you would probably say something like "Yes, I understand how you feel, but you can do it"; or "You're worth it!"; or "But you have your whole life ahead of you!"

Your biggest objection might be that you feel there is nothing you are good at. This is a very common though inaccurate perception for those who have a low self-image. For you, it might help to change the wording of this step to "find something you do *adequately!*" Adequate is fine. There's nothing wrong with being average.

Don't make the mistake of selling yourself short because you believe you are not good at anything. You're being too hard on yourself, and you may be making the mistake of thinking that unless you are *the best* at something, then you are no good *at all*. This kind of thinking can lead us into a dangerous perfectionism.

I remember a woman at one of our Fresh Start seminars for people recovering from divorce. She claimed that she was really not good at anything, and that she had done nothing but "wipe noses and bottoms for the past twelve years." Now she was in a dead-end job, barely making ends meet, and with little hope for the future.

I asked her about her strengths and interests, but she claimed she had none. She appeared to be quite depressed. I asked what she wanted to do with her life, and she had no idea. So I asked, "What did you want to do and

CHARACTERISTICS OF THE PERFECTIONIST

Striving to do well	**Striving to be perfect**
Focus on what is	Focus on what *should* be
Realistic	Idealistic
Accepts failure	Cannot accept failure
Motivated to succeed	Driven—"I *must* . . ."
It's okay to be average	Average is unacceptable
Desire to do my best	Always a demand
Want to do well for myself	Constant comparison to others
Self-image is more secure	"I will never measure up!"
Free to try again	Slave to constant effort
Life is a challenge	Life is a curse

what were you interested in before you got married?"

"That's a long time ago," she replied, "but I remember in college they told me I had a very logical and organized mind. I did okay in school but never graduated. Now I work as a receptionist/secretary, but have no marketable skills."

"Can you type?" I asked.

"Oh yeah, I can do that," she replied.

"Well, then, why don't you take a word processing class and learn some of the new software on a personal computer?"

With very little enthusiasm, she said she'd think about it.

I got a letter from the same lady about a year after our

meeting. She stated that she not only learned word processing, but also spreadsheets, programming, and some other things that I didn't understand. Subsequent letters stated that she had started her own data entry and word processing business in the basement of her home, and now she has six employees. Her letters are enthusiastic about the future of her business. She is obviously not the depressed lady that I had met several years earlier. This lady knows she has much more to offer than "wiping noses and bottoms."

We all have hidden talents and abilities that we could be using not only to better our lives, but also to give us a sense of competence and direction. Let's discover those gifts, find those open doors, and begin moving forward boldly.

I knew a young woman who was quite a good actress—but no one else knew it yet. Coming out of college, she tried to play it safe, getting an entry-level job in counseling (she had minored in psychology) and later pursuing a master's degree in teaching. While these seemed like sensible directions, she felt unhappy with herself. You see, she really wanted to act—not to teach it or think about it, but to do it.

So she took a bold step, dropping out of her master's program and beginning to audition for plays in New York City. It's a tough game there, with many competitors, and a year later she still hadn't landed any good jobs. So she moved to Chicago and auditioned there—with the same results. No one wanted to give her a chance to do what she knew she did best.

At that point I rather innocently suggested that she hire herself. "You've got friends who are in the same situation,"

I said. "Why don't you just get together and act? If that's what you do, do it. Don't wait for others to make it happen for you, make it happen for yourself!"

What did I know? But she took my advice. She formed a theater group that involved not only a handful of actors working together, but also instruction for children. It developed into a summer program for inner-city kids in a couple of different cities. She found some fulfillment in that, and later she did find regular acting work in Philadelphia.

My actress friend made some bold moves with her career. I admire her for that. She seized on something she could do well, and she pursued it. She faced distractions and obstacles, but pushed through them. Her life hasn't been easy, with no job security and meager pay. There were times when she was strongly tempted to drop it all. One temp job in New York could have become permanent, but she turned it down because it would have kept her from what she really wanted to do.

I know that there are lots of actors doggedly determined to "make it," but who really should be selling shoes or something—they just don't have the talent. They need to be more honest in their self-appraisal of strengths and weaknesses. They need to find experts who will be brutally forthright with them about their chances in that field. And that goes for many other fields as well. Determination is great, but not if you are following an obvious pipe dream.

Yet if you have accurately assessed your strengths, you need to choose an area and go for it. Get involved with groups that will help you do what you do best. Your step toward self-esteem will probably not mean pursuing a theater career—but it's possible that it might eventually involve some kind of career change. It might be something as simple as joining a church choir, or teaching a class in your specialty, or volunteering to help out in some way at a neighborhood center.

Choose Wisely

As you think about your assets, choose areas of interest and ability that have been with you or noticeable to others for more than a year. Don't choose to follow a dream you've only had for a short time, or jump from whim to whim. This will just leave you feeling confused and like a failure.

Recognize That Any Weakness Can Become an Asset

Immaturity can be turned into "a great sense of humor." Compulsiveness can become a "tremendous sense of responsibility." My own divorce, which was the greatest source of shame in my life, has become the greatest learning experience I've faced. I wouldn't wish it on my worst enemy, but I wouldn't trade anything for what it has taught me.

I believe the key is one's own attitude. Is this experience or weakness going to make me bitter or better? What do I need to learn from it? How can I bring my life into better balance?

Set Short- and Long-Term Goals for Your Life

Every business has to have a five- or ten-year plan. Then it needs to have specific goals and strategies for reaching its projected target. While I see the importance of doing that in my own business, I am very poor at it when it comes to my personal life. This usually reflects a lack of interest or direction for personal development.

Start by writing down where you would like to be in five or ten years. Make sure your goals are all things that are in your control—*not* "I want to be married in five years," but "I want to learn how to love others and to be committed in a relationship."

These goals can cover several areas: your personal finances, your family, your career, your spiritual life, and your friendships or relationships.

Then write specific plans or strategies for accomplishing those goals. What will it take for you to accomplish this? What will you need to do? You may need the help of others, such as friends or mentors. If your goal is something you know little about, you may want to find people who are already there and pick their brains a bit to find out what you need to do.

Choose an anniversary date for a review of these goals and your overall direction. I recommend a time that will be hard for you to forget, such as your birthday or New Year's Day. Then review your goals and your progress. Don't be surprised if you have to redo all of your strategies from time to time. My own five-year plan seems to change every six months. This is not a sign of failure but a sign that one is growing and changing. Some of your plans may be consistent throughout your whole life, but other things will change as you learn, develop, try new things, and explore new ideas.

Plan to Succeed

I know I have encouraged you to move forward boldly, but be careful about those first few steps, especially if you have not felt very successful for a while. You need to make sure your first step forward is a successful one, so make sure you choose something you know you can do. That may not seem very challenging. It isn't meant to be. The goal here is to get some motivation going. Once you are on your way, with a few small successes under your belt, a setback or two will not be as devastating. But if your first step forward is a perceived failure, you might not get started again for a long time.

For example, remember the lady at my seminar who said she couldn't do anything? I recommended that she take a class. If I were her counselor, her first goal might have been to find a course and sign up for it. This is only a "baby step," but in her condition it was all she needed to do at that point. This is something I knew she could do, and once she did it she would gain a sense of accomplishment and motivation for the next step. Her next step might have been merely to "show up for the first class."

Step by step the healing happens. Step by step you discover who you are and why you're so important.

CHAPTER 10

The Human Touch

Self-love was the major movement of the 1970s. Falling in love with yourself is easy—the hard part is breaking up.
—ALEX AYRES, FROM *THE WIT AND WISDOM OF MARK TWAIN*

I always wanted to be somebody, but I should have been more specific.
—LILY TOMLIN

Grace, 73, was confined to a hospital bed. My colleague Tom Jones tells of his first pastoral visit to see her. Physically, she was a wreck, crippled by arthritis. Her joints were fused, her limbs twisted. If anyone had reason to feel down on herself, it was this woman.

Tom arrived in the hospital room with Grace's daughter.

"The pastor is here to see you," the daughter said.

Grace was lying with her back toward the door. "Come over here where I can see you," she piped up. Already, Tom could sense a spritely spirit in her.

Tom moved around the bed and Grace took a good look. With a twinkle in her eye, she said, "You're not as bad-looking as everyone says." Tom knew he had a friend.

Nurses told Tom that if there was an especially crabby patient, they'd put her in Grace's room. Within no time at all, Grace would engage these complainers in conversation, and before long they were much happier and beginning to adopt Grace's optimistic outlook on life.

Life had dealt Grace a bad hand, and she might seem justified in hating herself, hating her condition. But instead she reached out in love to others. Her body was crippled, but her spirit soared.

The person who moves or acts* gracefully *has a rhythm going on. There is a grateful receiving of the gift of movement, and a gracious expression of that movement toward others. Strutting or preening is not graceful—it is self-centered, not receiving or giving. Graceful movement has both the confidence of a gift received and the humility of a gift given to others.

The secret to the next step on the road to becoming your own best friend is *grace*—giving out what you have received. As you get involved in the lives of others, you will find purpose and joy for your own life.

Step 8: Get Involved in the Lives of Others.

Psychologists have cited the two greatest emotional needs of human beings as *security* and *significance*. We have discussed the first need, the need for security, when we talked about our need for unconditional love. We are secure only when we know that we are loved for who we are, and that love will not fade over time or circumstances.

This step will explore the second area of emotional need—the search for significance. We feel significant when we know that we have made an impact on others, that their lives have been improved or made fuller by our existence.

We feel significant when we know that we have made an impact on others. Investing in tasks is the first step in finding significance, but ultimately tasks are not enough. We must move to the next step: investing our lives in the lives of others.

In step 7, I talked about my own recovery from divorce. As I pointed out, part of my healing was in finding what I was good at and then doing it to the best of my abilities. Our search for significance begins by investing in *tasks*. We can invest ourselves in our education, our jobs, our homes, cars, or hobbies. This can be very helpful to our self-image, as we discover and employ our God-given abilities. But ultimately tasks are not enough. We must move to the next step, investing our lives in the lives of others.

If you feel that you have nothing to offer, join a tutoring program in the inner city. Even your limited knowledge of English or math can help a needy kid or adult. If you don't feel that you can do anything, find others who feel the same way and encourage them.

From time to time, I'll organize a support group of clients who are facing similar issues. There's a fascinating dynamic in such groups. In a normal counseling set-up, I am the helper and my clients are the helped. But in these groups, the clients help each other. Sometimes I don't even need to be there. The most valuable things that are said come from the members of the group.

"I know. That happened to me once."

"I used to feel like that, but then I . . ."

"No, you're not weird to think that way. A lot of people think that way."

"I'm still struggling with those issues. You're not alone."

Not only does each person get the benefit of six or eight "counselors" instead of just one, but group members can be of help to each other. They can use their struggles for some good. Their own burdens can lighten the burden on someone else.

Brendan had suffered a devastating breakup with a girlfriend. His self-esteem was in the pits. The emotional pain was so great, he wondered why God could allow him to go through that.

But a few months after the breakup, Brendan was talking with a friend—who had just been dumped by a girlfriend. Brendan was able to comfort this friend because he had been there. "I know what to say now," Brendan told me. "Before my own breakup, I never would have known what to say. But suddenly it was as if it all had meaning. I didn't mind having to go through all that pain, if I could use my experience to comfort others."

As we were coming up with the wording for this step, we considered saying, "Use your strengths to help others."

Obviously, once you've identified your strengths, you should use these in the tasks you choose (step 7) or the people you invest in (step 8). But then we realized that we don't just help people with our strengths. We help them with our weaknesses, too.

This can be a tremendously freeing idea. Think about it: You don't have to be perfect to make a difference in someone else's life. In fact, sometimes your *struggles* are your best credentials.

A person who is facing poor self-esteem can read a million books from distant authors saying "Feel good about yourself." But all those words pale in value next to the simple encouragement of a fellow sufferer coming alongside and saying, "I know. I feel that way sometimes, too. But you really are very special."

Getting Involved: A Primer

So how do you do this? It sounds easy enough: Invest in someone's life. But what does that mean?

Be There

Most of us want to say the right thing or do the right thing to solve someone's problems, but healthy investment starts with *presence*. Just be there. In the book of Job, we read of three friends of the famous sufferer who sat with him on the trash heap for a week without speaking. When they started speaking, *that's* when they got in trouble.

Many fathers (and some mothers) fail to recognize the value of mere presence. They try to make up for a lack of "quantity time" with "quality time." To a point, this works—but parents need to be accessible to their kids, to be there playing, laughing, and just living.

Step one in relationship-building is just being there. Being at the football game. Being at the school play. Being at the snack bar. Being available for phone calls.

As you begin to invest in someone's life, don't ignore the obvious. Be there for them.

I remember when I went through my divorce how my friends all seemed to disappear. When I would run into them years later, they would usually apologize and say something about not knowing what to say. I would tell them, "Just calling and saying* that *would have been enough."

Listen

Take the time to pay attention to the person. I'm talking about *active* listening here. Ask questions to draw out the other person. Be interested in that person's life.

Comedian Paula Poundstone was recently on a talk show complaining about her own lack of listening skills. She talks too much about herself, she says. She told of a conversation with Barbara Walters, who had just interviewed the President. "What was it like?" Poundstone asked. (So far, so good; active listening.)

Walters began to describe her arrival at the White House and Poundstone interrupted, "Oh, I toured the White House once. That's really lovely, isn't it?" This would best be described as "selfish listening." That's when we listen to what others say and merely reflect on how it relates to us and our lives. Walters had a wonderful story to tell, and Poundstone was thinking only of herself.

The comedian mused about what might have happened if she had ever met with Martin Luther King, Jr. He'd say, "I have a dream!" and she'd say, "Oh, I had a dream once . . ."

Do not compare yourself with other people, but listen and engage them in their self-revelation.

Trust. Trust is another key component of personal communication. The other person needs to trust you, and that means you need to be trustworthy. Confidential matters must be kept confidential. A person needs to learn that he or she can tell you things without being judged or hated. So listening carries a great responsibility.

You may be frustrated because you're ready to listen, but the other person isn't ready to share anything significant. Be patient. It doesn't mean you're doing anything wrong. Trust can take a while to develop.

Share Yourself in a Balanced Way

"Balance" is the key word here. A relationship in which one person talks all the time while the other listens is out of balance. As you truly listen to someone else, you will find the opportunity to open up about yourself.

Paula Poundstone's strategy was not that bad. It is a good idea to share things from your own life—but of course she was out of balance. Don't be afraid to share your own thoughts and needs and feelings, as long as the other person is encouraging you to do so.

The trust issue works both ways. You need to trust the other person, and that may take some time. Sharing yourself with others will require you to take some risks. But once you have learned to like yourself, taking calculated risks will become a much easier process.

Learning to become your own best friend will also allow you to take greater risks in relationships.

Put Yourself in Others' Shoes

Allow yourself to see others' point of view. You don't have to agree with them on every issue, but at least try to understand why they think as they do.

I know a woman who has bad luck with relationships. Boyfriends, friends, co-workers—there's a long list of people she has severed connections with because, she says, they've mistreated her. In some cases, I know it's true—she *has* been used.

But I'm coming to the conclusion that she has misread many of these other relationships. I believe she is self-centered. Not selfish—she is actually a very caring and giving person. But she has not learned to put herself in the shoes of the other person, to give that person the benefit of the doubt. This is not a moral problem as much as a problem of perspective. She has a great heart for people, but she needs to relax her self-centered fears and see through someone else's eyes.

This sort of empathy is a crucial ingredient in healthy relationships.

People who tend to consistently take the role of victim may in fact be self-centered. Their

eyes are only on their hurts, their life, and how everything that happens affects them.

Establish Your Boundaries and Stick to Them

Junior got his spelling test back with just one mistake. "Junior," the teacher said, "I thought you said you knew how to spell all these words. But here you spelled *banana* 'B-A-N-A-N-A-N-A.'"

Junior thought quickly and said, "Well, I know how to spell it. I just don't know when to stop."

Many people—especially those with low self-esteem—have no problem feeling empathy in a relationship. They just don't know when to stop.

This is an easy direction to take if you have little sense of your own value. If your *only* purpose in life is to help this other person, then you will easily give up your own rights, your own needs, even your own well-being to do so. That's not healthy.

Many professional caregivers fall into this trap. And it is more common among women (who are trained from an early age to find their value in relationships) than among men. As I mentioned earlier, I had to set boundaries in my counseling work when I felt it began to dominate my life.

People helpers have a high rate of burn-out. This is prevalent in those who have not learned to set proper boundaries in their efforts to help others.

As you reach out to others in relationships, especially if you are doing something to help them, be very careful not to violate your own boundaries. Be sure that this person is not dominating your time or your energy or your feelings. You may even want to set rules at some point about how much time you spend with this person, or how far you will go to help.

And you will probably feel guilty about setting these boundaries. I've talked with my fellow counselors here in my office about this same issue. We all struggle to set proper boundaries for ourselves, and we often feel that we should do more to help people. But then we reassure ourselves (and each other) that we will only be able to *continue* helping others if we set reasonable limits on our current efforts.

Respect the Other Person's Boundaries

Sometimes in our efforts to help others, we can do for them what they should be doing for themselves. We can take over their lives.

Of course, this doesn't really help them very much. Just as you need to set boundaries for yourself, you need to respect the boundaries of others. Do not make their decisions for them. Do not seek to make yourself indispensable to them. Try to strengthen them as much as possible.

Many new therapists, in their efforts to help others, will do all the work for the client. They call repeatedly to schedule appointments, check on them frequently, and help with excuses when no work is done. One of the greatest predictors of counseling success is the *clients'* motivation to help themselves.

This is a tricky thing. We are suggesting that "getting involved in the lives of others" can be a step toward finding your own value. And certainly these relationships can help you to realize your own significance. But your sense of personal value must not *depend* on another person. You are valuable all by yourself. You can use that value in relationships. You can use that value to help others. But those relationships are not the source of your worth. When you begin to place your whole self-esteem in an individual relationship, you invariably put too much pressure on the relationship. Either it will fall to pieces, or it will melt into something unhealthy.

This is illustrated in our relationships with our own children. While it is perfectly appropriate for a mother to dress a three year old, you are only handicapping the child if you continue this into adolescence. I suspect that parents who "over-parent" are usually meeting more of their own needs than the needs of their children.

Move Carefully Toward Commitment

In a way, commitment is happening from the first moments of a relationship. I commit myself to look at you. You commit yourself to see me and nod. In that most casual of transactions, we commit ourselves to regard each other as human beings.

When I ask about your health, or your work, or your opinion of the Philadelphia Phillies, I am committing myself to listen to your answer. And as you answer, you are entrusting me with some knowledge of yourself.

Step by step, boundaries are being crossed. At the start, these are easily crossable boundaries. I may have a boundary of not talking to people on the commuter train, but this affable guy beside me seems friendly enough; I'll commit myself to a conversation with him.

Commitment is a redefinition of boundaries.

If you were to go to a stranger on the street, slap him on the back, and say, "How ya doin'?" it would be inappropriate. You would be crossing boundaries. And yet you might do the same thing to a friend. What's the difference? You have made some sort of commitment. You have redrawn your boundary lines to include slaps on the back as acceptable behavior.

But could you say "I need to stay at your house tonight?"

Or "I have to confess to you about something terrible I've done"?

In most casual friendships, such statements would cross the line. But as relationships progress, commitments are made, the lines are redrawn. In committed relationships, you can count on a place to stay, you can offer unsolicited opinions on personal matters, you can be open about your needs and failings. Not that you ever specifically negotiate these things, or hammer out a contract to determine the boundaries of your level of commitment. These things just evolve.

My co-author, Randy, was recently involved in a concert at his church. He invited two friends to come and see it. He had attended various shows that they had been in, but he had not invited them to any specific event at his church. Until now.

The friends did come to the concert. In so doing, they confirmed their commitment, as friends, to Randy. Essentially they were saying, "You can count on us to support you in things that are important to you, just as you have supported us in our important activities." Nothing was said, but a tiny step of friendship-commitment was made.

For many, marriage is the most committed relationship

they could have. But there are also close friendships that are very committed. Such relationships are therapeutic. They build us up. If you can move toward some level of mutual commitment in a healthy relationship, do it. But maintain your self-defining boundaries.

In commitment, the boundary lines are *redrawn* but not *erased*. Even in a marriage, there must be healthy boundaries of personhood. And such redefinition happens slowly, in stages.

I know people—I'm sure you do too—who have fallen in love at first sight. They commit to each other very quickly, and they're married within months. In most cases, these turn out to be rocky relationships. They are left with a need to redefine their boundaries after they have already made the commitment. Good commitment happens step by step. Don't rush it.

This also happens in situations of help and ministry. I have found that some clients, after pouring out their heart to me in a session, expect me to be their closest friend. I need to be very clear on the boundaries in this counselor–client relationship. But sometimes it's the help*er* who rushes into a commitment, such as a volunteer who begins to tutor an inner-city child and expects instant love and devotion in return.

You may find, as you begin to invest your life in the lives of others, that you are rushing into a commitment of some kind, or that the other person is. Slow down. Stick to your boundaries. Let the commitment happen naturally, in its time.

In commitment, the boundary lines are redrawn but not erased. Even in marriage,

there must be healthy boundaries of personhood. Healthy commitment happens step by step. Don't rush it.

As we move forward through step 8, getting involved in the lives of others, we will find that very few of these relationships will lead to a committed, loving union. And this must never be our goal. In my work at divorce recovery conferences, I come across many who get involved in helping others in order to "meet someone special" (although they might not admit it). I tell them that they are not ready to be remarried until they don't *need* to be remarried. In other words, your search for significance is not found in a relationship with someone who is going to fulfill you or complete your life. You need to be a whole person, someone who has learned to be content right where you are, before you can reach out for a committed, loving relationship. Become your own best friend before you consider a marriage or remarriage relationship.

Grace found her significance in reaching out to others. At age 73, and with limited health, she was still able to make a dramatic impact on those around her. Her self-image was not based on temporal things such as outward beauty, but on the strength of her inner character. I hope I can be that healthy when I'm her age.

CHAPTER 11

Keeping Your Balance

The greatest discovery of my generation is that a human being can alter his life by altering his attitudes of mind.
—WILLIAM JAMES (1842–1910)

What happens when you've gone through all the steps? You have chased down the villains, discovered your strengths, and restructured your ways of thinking—then what? Are you "healed"? Can you throw away your crutches and waltz through the rest of life?

Maybe. But it's very likely that the struggle will continue. You may have gained the upper hand, but those feelings of inadequacy are pesky things. They arise at the most inopportune moments. You'll be sailing along in a good spirit, and—*wham!*—some experience or crisis or comment will knock you to the dust. You'll need to go back and do your homework all over again. Expect this. Unless you are especially blessed, it will happen to you.

HINTS ON MAINTAINING A BEST FRIENDSHIP WITH YOURSELF

• Start each day with prayer and meditation about your relationship with God. Recognize your value as part of his creation, and celebrate the gifts he has given you. Pray for strength and wisdom as you go through each day.

• When you examine your life, do so with a mirror and not a magnifying glass. Don't put yourself down or exaggerate your weaknesses. Make sure you treat yourself with the same care and compassion that you would extend to a best friend.

• Identify and then seek contact with those friends who build you up. Recognize the importance of those relationships and determine to help each other understand the value of self and others.

• Graciously accept compliments and learn to honestly encourage others by complimenting them.

• View your mistakes as opportunities to learn, to grow, and to improve yourself.

• Find your own "garden of joy." What do you really enjoy? Elegant dinners? A sauna? Fishing all by yourself? Determine to treat yourself to this activity at least once a month. You're worth it.

• Regularly examine your self-talk and realign it toward the truth. Reject perfectionism and endless "should" statements.

• Set short- and long-term goals that challenge and stretch you. Work on self-improvement without self-condemnation. Don't compare yourself with others, but honestly seek areas where you would like to grow.

• Improve your surroundings. Straighten up the clutter, clean a room or two, get some plants or flowers. Your attitude will be more pleasant as your environment improves.

• Learn to relax and enjoy life without feeling guilty. If you don't feel it, force yourself to do it anyway. Tell yourself that you deserve it. In time you won't have to fake it anymore. Hopefully, this attitude will become part of your lifestyle.

Step 9: Adopt This New Way of Thinking About Yourself as Part of an Ongoing Lifestyle.

Even in my counseling practice, with all of the therapists I know, we find ourselves doing regular maintenance of our self-image. Sure, we're supposed to have it all together; and we're supposed to be the ones who are challenging others to become their own best friends. But the truth is that we also struggle and need to remind ourselves of these principles on a regular basis.

Maintenance is now the key concept. Those jolts will happen, but you can fortify yourself so that they don't affect you as much. If you plan wisely, you will not fall back as far or as often.

Regular auto maintenance is a good analogy to use as you seek to keep your balance. You don't need to be obsessive about getting positive strokes from everyone you meet, but you shouldn't "let yourself go" either. Plan regular evaluation of your self-esteem level, and if you're sliding, go to the people or activities you need to keep yourself filled up.

Many of the maintenance strategies we'll suggest here will sound familiar. They are spinoffs of some of the same tactics we've been discussing throughout this book. But regular attention to these matters will help bolster you and keep you out of trouble zones.

Just as with your car, regular maintenance of your self-image is far more effective than having to make major repairs.

Know Your Down Times

Most people have certain rhythms to their levels of self-esteem. These may be determined by your schedule, the people around you, or even your body chemistry. If you know when your self-esteem will be most threatened, you can guard yourself. Plan to be with supportive people in those times. Do not schedule high-risk activities.

For many women, monthly menstrual cycles take them on an emotional roller coaster. At certain points in their hormonal changes, everything they encounter has a heightened effect. Thus, attacks on their self-esteem can be especially damaging at these times. If this is regularly a problem for you, prepare for it by reducing your stress-producing activities and gathering the support resources you need.

For some people, their rises and dips in self-esteem follow a job schedule—every Monday, for instance, might be a down time. Or after every Tuesday's executive meeting. For some churchgoers, Sunday can be a down time. For others, it's an up time, but by Saturday their tank is running low. Maybe there's a regular activity that gets you down; some might have a self-esteem crisis just after they work out at the gym, or when they watch a certain TV show.

Monitor your self-esteem. Try to deduce a pattern in your ups and downs. And then prepare yourself for the down times.

Know Your Trouble People

Just as you have down times, you have trouble people. These are not necessarily the "villains" of your past (though they may be). And they don't necessarily try to make you feel insecure. They just do.

For many people, it's parents. No matter how old they are, such people still feel like little kids when they're around their parents. Perhaps some old patterns from childhood creep into the relationship.

It could be a friend or acquaintance you tend to be jealous of, or that co-worker who puts you down all the time. For some divorced people I know, it's the ex-spouse who sends them reeling every other weekend when they transfer the kids.

Again, monitor yourself. Figure out which people cause trouble for your self-esteem. Then:

- avoid them; or
- just avoid them during your down times; or
- prepare for them by bolstering your self-image in advance; or at least
- make up for them with some solid support from others afterward.

It's possible that you could redeem some of these relationships by talking things out with these people or by doing some major self-talk. But it's also possible that you never will feel entirely right in their presence. In this case, you just have to cope—avoid, fortify, or heal.

Take Care of Yourself

I'm talking about simple physical care here. You know the drill:

- Don't work too hard.
- Eat regular meals.
- Make sure you're getting proper nutrition.
- Get enough sleep.
- Exercise regularly.
- Respond to your body's warning signals.

"Yeah, yeah, yeah." You've been getting this pitch since the second grade. But you probably don't realize how these simple behaviors can affect your self-esteem.

My co-author, Randy, provides the case study here. He's been working hard on this book—and on a dozen other projects in his free-lance career. All the deadlines landed at once, and he has had a stress-filled time, working too hard to get these projects done.

Exercise is the first to go. Randy has a health-club membership, but he's been too busy lately to take advantage of it. Then meals got shoved aside. He'd work through lunch, then get hungry and snack at 4 P.M. Then he'd be hungry again at 10 P.M., which is a terrible time to eat. He'd starve himself for a while, then pig out. And then he wondered why he felt so fat. Does this sound familiar at all?

Next, his sleep patterns went awry. He'd work late at night, or come home from some activity and crash in front of the TV. Sometimes he'd try to sleep late, but the morning light caused a fitful, inefficient sleep, so he'd still wake up tired.

In situations like this, a spiral effect kicks in. One breakdown of personal discipline led to another, and Randy, who normally has fine self-esteem, began to doubt himself. That, of course, made him work less efficiently, which intensified the pressure, which robbed him of sleep, nutrition, and so on. He's doing better now, thank you. But still, he's glad this is the last chapter.

Be careful not to let these simple physical patterns of your life slip away. Sure, you can get by on a day or two of below-par eating or sleeping. But beware of the snowball effect.

Find a Support System

You need people who will lift you up. You need people you can call when you need encouragement.

This may start with just one other person, a friend who understands you. But try to expand that source of support by finding a few others. In a supportive group, you will find:

- *Listening ears*—people to hear your gripes and needs;
- *Encouragement*—they'll assure you of your value and let you know you're not alone;
- *Accountability*—group members can "check up on you" in nonthreatening ways; if your expectations are out of line, they'll tell you;
- *Practical assistance*—if you need a job, or a ride, or a loan, or someone to watch the kids, or a place to stay, or a good book, the group may come through for you;
- *A place to be somebody*—if you're feeling like a nobody, a group of friends can give you a sense of belonging;
- *Other needy people to help*—you can gain a greater

sense of significance as you, in turn, give others the support they need.

I know a church singles group that provides its members with a much-needed support system. It's not large—most of its meetings have only eight or ten attending. But the members are enriched through their interaction with each other.

In the two years this group has met, it has helped members deal with divorces, broken romances, financial crises, job changes, deaths in the family, addictive tendencies, and various spiritual questions. People feel free to communicate their needs. No one claims perfection. All are fellow strugglers.

Several group members struggle with self-esteem, *but they're getting better*. It helps to have the group say, "We're glad you're here." It helps to know that you contribute something unique to the group. It helps to know that people are praying for you.

You may find such a group at a church or through a community organization or a counselor's office. Or you may be able to pull together a group of friends and start your own. You don't need eight or ten. Two or three would be fine. But get the support you need.

Accept Your Limits

You can't do everything. You can't be what everyone wants you to be. You will fail at some things—we all do. Once you understand your own strengths and weaknesses, and accept them both, you will free yourself from all sorts of self-condemnation.

My colleague Vince Gallagher tells of a man he knew.

The man was pastor of a church, but he was miserable. He was convinced that he was failing in his work; he just lacked the people skills to succeed in ministry. Vince saw the man again a few years later, and the man was quite happy with his life. He had quit the pastorate and started to work with computers. It was a very different job, but one that utilized his gifts better.

Was this man a failure? Not at all. He got to a point where he realized he was in the wrong job. He accepted the fact that he lacked certain skills—and had others. There's no disgrace in that!

Another colleague of mine, Cheryl Smith, said it this way, "I recently had to come to the realization that I was not going to get my doctorate, and I wasn't going to write a book. I know that I have plenty of other strengths that I can build on, but realizing and accepting the limits of how far I could go in my career gave me the freedom to begin exploring more realistic expectations."

As I said earlier, I'm a bad speller. I know it, accept it, and allow for it. Whatever your limitations are, do not begrudge them. Do not let them bring down your overall sense of self. You don't have to succeed totally, in every aspect of life, to be a success.

Celebrate Your Strengths

Along the same lines, you can boost your self-esteem by becoming aware of your strengths and focusing on those.

If you'll allow another sports analogy, let me bring up the case of baseball slugger Mike Schmidt. I remember several years ago when Schmidt decided he wanted to hit for a high batting average. To do this, he needed to get lots of little hits, not just the booming home runs he was known for. He worked on this avidly and had a little success with it—but he wasn't hitting as many home runs. Finally, the manager went to him and said, "We appreciate your wanting to be a 'total' hitter and to get all these hits. But we have other players who hit singles. We need you to hit home runs." Schmidt needed to celebrate his strengths instead of concentrating on his weakness.

We faced a similar situation in our counseling office. One of our counselors was complaining that she often felt inadequate because she didn't have as much formal education as the other counselors in our office. She worried that her clients might be short-changed because she didn't have the book-knowledge to pinpoint their problems.

The fact is that this counselor is an excellent listener. She has a quality that no school can teach you—empathy. She more than makes up for her lesser education with her uncanny ability to understand the precise emotions of her clients. She needs to celebrate this strength and to place more confidence in it, rather than put herself down for what she does not have.

Separate Your Core Self from Risky Tasks

You need to take some risks. But hedge your bets. Don't let your whole sense of self ride on a risky endeavor.

Sometimes people with poor self-esteem will stop taking risks. They feel they'll probably fail anyway, so why try? This is not good. We need to keep trying new things.

But others take unwise risks, and they invest too much in them. A man decides to go all out to woo a woman he just met. An actress decides to move to Hollywood and try to break into films. An accountant quits his job to write the great American novel. A churchgoer decides to conquer stage fright by singing a difficult aria in front of the whole congregation.

These people are like the compulsive gambler who bets his whole bundle on a long shot. The stakes are high and the odds are against them. It would be better to try tasks that are less risky. The wooer should start with a friendship, the actress with community theater. The accountant should keep his day job and the singer should join the choir first.

But the other approach to risk-taking is to shield your core self from those risks. Be sure to separate your own self-worth from this particular task. You must get to the point of saying "If I fail, it's no great loss. It does not mean I'm not a good person. At least I tried."

This reminds me of my dating days. When I was emotionally vulnerable, or when my self-image was at risk, I would not ask a girl out unless it was a sure thing. I couldn't risk the chance that she might say no. But as I grew in self-confidence, I would ask myself this question before calling a new prospect—"What will happen to me if she says *no?*"

If my answer to myself was "I'd be disappointed, but I'd be fine with that," then I'd make the call. But if my answer sounded anything like "I'd be crushed!," then I knew not to take the risk.

That may go against every positive-thinking book on the market, but it's an essential strategy for all of us seeking to maintain a healthy self-esteem—*prepare to fail (at risky tasks)*. Do not set yourself up to crash. Have a crash plan in effect.

Take some risks, but be smart about it. Don't bet your whole self-image on a long shot, and don't take any risk that could threaten your core self.

Rewrite Your Personal Script

Have you ever found yourself saying or doing certain things and then later wondering why? Sometimes it's as if someone else has written a script for you, and you're just saying the lines.

Often you may think, "That wasn't me. That was my mother saying those things." Or "It was like I *became* my father when I did that."

If you don't know what I'm talking about, just move on to the next section. It's not any sort of mystical experience, it's just the programming of our past. There are certain "voices" we hear, certain expectations and equations.

You need to write your own script.

Recently the TV series *L.A. Law* changed its writers. The show had gotten too crazy. It had left the basic approach that had originally made it popular. So the old writers were out and new writers were in. That's the kind of coup I'm talking about here. You are the one who decides how you are going to live. Throw out the other scriptwriters and create your own story line.

How? By talking to yourself. Psychologists call it "self-talk." You might think that is a sign of insanity, but it's actually a proven way to stay sane in the midst of the various pressures around us. Books have been written about it, and some of them are quite helpful.

Simply, self-talk involves listening for the bad messages in your head and correcting them. Replace them with new messages that *you* choose. How do you want to think about yourself? Get into the habit of telling yourself these good things.

"You can't do it. Don't even try."

"You're such an embarrassment."

"Why can't you be as good as your sister?"

These are some of the messages that may afflict you. In the privacy of your own mind, argue with them.

"I *can* do this. At least it's worth a try."

"I am worth a lot. I'm not an embarrassment."

"I don't need to compare myself to anyone."

Through the habit of positive self-talk, you can rewrite your personal script in new and exciting ways.

I know that some of my fellow Christians might be hesitant to adopt a psychological technique such as self-talk, but the Bible also talks about "renewing your minds" (see Rom. 12:2). This is done by getting rid of the old, sinful thoughts and beginning to view yourself the way God views you.

Of the two sample messages above, which sounds more God-honoring? As a Christian, I believe that we are in a spiritual battle for our minds. I believe that "the enemy" wants to defeat us and fill our minds with lies that discourage us and keep us doubting ourselves. God, however, is a God of truth and grace. Talking to ourselves includes rejecting the lies from the enemy, and focusing on the truths from God's Word. Let me suggest, then, that you battle those negative voices with prayer and verses about how we are his children, how he delights in us, and how we are "fearfully and wonderfully made" (see Ps. 139:14).

Each time you find your life being "scripted" by those voices from the past, ask God for the power to be all that he wants you to be. Thank him for creating you and redeeming you. Let *him* write your life script.

Accept Your Enemies

To paraphrase Lincoln, "You can please some of the people all the time, and you can please all the people some of the time, but you can't please all the people all the time."

I am a people-pleaser. I want to make people happy. It bothers me when people don't like me. I want to search out the problem and make things right. In my role as president of Fresh Start and Life Counseling Services, I sometimes find myself being easier on people than I should be. I'm a pushover because I want my co-workers to like me, my clients to like me, and all my business associates to like me.

Part of maintaining your self-esteem is accepting the fact that not everyone will like you. There will be some who disagree with you on crucial issues. There will be some who are offended by what you do. There will be some who just don't like your style. You must learn to live with that.

Your value as a person does not rest on other people's opinions. God does not run a popularity poll on each person to determine whether or not he loves you.

Certainly you don't want to offend people needlessly. You *should* care for other people. If people have legitimate gripes against you, hear them out and make things right. But there may be some matters that you will never be able to overcome. Some people will be your enemies despite your best efforts to make them friends. You must learn to wash your hands of these problems.

As a manager of people, I've learned that sometimes I have to make unpopular decisions. People will not like my choices. And sometimes they may decide not to like me. I can take reasonable steps to explain my position and to listen to their problem, but there's only so much I can do. I need to move on with my life and work.

Avoid the "New Math" of Self-Definition

Some of the negative self-talk messages that keep coming up are almost mathematical in nature. As we seek to define ourselves, to measure our worth, there are all sorts of unhealthy equations that come to mind.

Greater Than/Less Than. You've heard this, I'm sure. "Why can't you be as _____ as _____?" Fill in the blanks. Blank A might include: pretty, smart, talented, caring, sweet, popular, interesting. Blank B might be full of your competitors: brothers and sisters, parents, classmates, teammates, TV stars.

We live in a highly competitive world. The comparisons will fly around you daily. Don't fall into that trap. Remember that you are in a league by yourself. Each of us has individual gifts and abilities. Comparisons are moot.

Equals. Watch out for definitions that limit you to one specific aspect of your life.

"I am my job." If you don't succeed at work, climbing the corporate ladder to realize your career goals, you are nothing. So goes this faulty logic. But work is just one part of a large life. Don't limit yourself.

"I am what my kids do." There's dangerous co-dependency in this statement, but many parents feel this way. If your kids turn out badly, if they're not the lawyers or doctors or missionaries you wanted them to be, you've failed. This doesn't work either. Your children make their own choices at a certain age. They become independent, and so should you.

"I am my looks." Many people place great emphasis on how they look. Look good, feel good—that's the way people live. A Gallup poll showed that 38 percent of Americans consider physical attractiveness "very important" to happiness and getting ahead. (Another 46 percent said "somewhat important.") So if you're having a bad-hair day, or a bad-face month, or a bad-hips year, you're not worth much. Hogwash! There is so much more to you than physical appearance. Don't get conned by this false equation.

Subtraction. In some situations, we tend to subtract value from our lives.

"If I am not perfect, I am not anything." Perfectionism is a cruel tyrant, and an illogical one. Don't fall into the "all or nothing" trap. Be happy with the "something" you have.

"If I am not in a romantic relationship, I am worth nothing." This is an axiom of the romance addict. It is also illogical and dangerous. Such people cannot see any value in themselves alone, but must get affirmation from a lover. This can lead to bad, desperate relationships, and even good relationships can crumble from the pressure. Romance can be good and wonderful, but even that is just a part of who you are. Don't put all your eggs in that basket.

Make Life and Lifestyle Decisions That Will Help Your Self-Esteem

As you seek to maintain your self-esteem, you may need to make some tough decisions. If self-esteem is a priority for you, you may need to give up a job or a relationship that continually threatens your self-esteem.

I don't say this lightly. I know that jobs are hard to come by. So are relationships, sometimes. The point is that your priorities may need to shift. Instead of asking "How much does this job pay?," you might want to ask "How well does this job use my God-given abilities?" Instead of "I like this beautiful person," it might be "This person makes me feel valuable."

Certainly self-esteem issues are not your only criteria, but they deserve a hearing.

A friend just told me about a decision he has made. He's an acting teacher, and every so often he gets invited to schools to hold theater seminars. He's fine with teenagers, but he just doesn't feel comfortable with younger kids. He agonizes over those seminars and usually comes away feeling pretty bad about his abilities as a teacher. Well, he has just made the obvious choice: he is going to say no to seminars with younger kids. Those seminars just aren't worth it. Other people could do them better and he doesn't need the pressure. He may lose a little income, but his self-esteem is worth the trade-off.

Seek to Develop Self-Esteem in Others

Pass it on. You can be a fountain of self-esteem for all those around you.

We tend to be so quick with the put-down. The casual

insult is part of our normal conversation. We should be more careful. We should seek to build others up as much as possible. Tell others how much you treasure them. Express how much you appreciate their specific abilities. As we develop these habits in our conversation, we can change the tone of our workplaces, our homes, our churches. Guaranteed.

The problem with many of the self-esteem books of the past is the one-way selfishness they promoted. Me first. Me only. I must stand up for my rights.

But there is a better way. As we truly appreciate the people we are, as God has made us, we won't need to fight for our self-worth. We can extend appreciation to others freely. It's not a zero-sum game. We can esteem others *and esteem ourselves*. In fact, we must.

How can we give to anyone else if we're convinced we have nothing of value to give? How can we truly love others without knowing how to properly love ourselves? How can we become our own best friend?

Review the steps we've presented. Continue to work on those areas where you are still weak. And remember to maintain what you have built.

Take a step toward becoming your own best friend. Then take another step. And another. Stay on this path and you will discover a life of love—for God, for others, and for yourself.

APPENDIX

In this Appendix we are offering two tests for you to consider taking as part of your own search to understand yourself better. The first test is a Personal Style Analysis. If you take it and have us score it for you, we will provide a six-page computer printout of your personality style, the way in which you prefer to relate to others, as well as some strengths and weaknesses.

The second survey provides an analysis of your Personal Interests and Values, or what motivates you. You will receive a six-page computer analysis of your interests and values as they pertain to the economic, aesthetic, social, political, and relational areas of your life.

Please make copies of the tests as you need them, and then send the answer sheet(s) to our offices.

Life Counseling Services
63 Chestnut Rd., Paoli, PA 19301
215-644-6464

Cost. The cost for each test is $15.00, which includes shipping and handling. You will receive a computer printout of about six pages for each answer sheet you send.

PERSONAL STYLE ANALYSIS

Ten Minutes That May Change Your Life

Directions

There are 24 groups of words listed here that describe personal style. Each group contains 4 lines of words. For each group select the line of words that best describes you. Place an ☒ in the box in the MOST column for that line. Then select the line of words that least describes your style in that group. Place an ☒ in the box next to that line in the LEAST column. Repeat this process in the remaining 23 word groups.

Refer to example below before proceeding:

Example:

M L
☒ ☐ Gentle, kindly
☐ ☒ Persuasive, convincing
☐ ☐ Humble, reserved, modest
☐ ☐ Original, inventive, individualistic

NAME ______________________ ADDRESS ______________________

PHONE (w) ______________ (h) ______________ MALE _____ FEMALE _____

M L **1** ☐ ☐ Gentle, kindly ☐ ☐ Persuasive, convincing ☐ ☐ Humble, reserved, modest ☐ ☐ Original, inventive, individualistic	M L **5** ☐ ☐ Jovial, joking ☐ ☐ Precise, exact ☐ ☐ Nervy, gutsy, brazen ☐ ☐ Even-tempered, calm, not easily excited
2 ☐ ☐ Attractive, charming, attracts others ☐ ☐ Cooperative, agreeable ☐ ☐ Stubborn, unyielding ☐ ☐ Sweet, pleasing	**6** ☐ ☐ Competitive, seeking to win ☐ ☐ Considerate, caring, thoughtful ☐ ☐ Outgoing, fun loving, socially striving ☐ ☐ Harmonious, agreeable
3 ☐ ☐ Easily led, follower ☐ ☐ Bold, daring ☐ ☐ Loyal, faithful, devoted ☐ ☐ Charming, delightful	**7** ☐ ☐ Fussy, hard to please ☐ ☐ Obedient, will do as told, dutiful ☐ ☐ Unconquerable, determined ☐ ☐ Playful, frisky, full of fun
4 ☐ ☐ Open-minded, receptive ☐ ☐ Obliging, helpful ☐ ☐ Willpower, strong willed ☐ ☐ Cheerful, joyful	**8** ☐ ☐ Brave, unafraid, courageous ☐ ☐ Inspiring, stimulating, motivating ☐ ☐ Submissive, yielding, gives in ☐ ☐ Timid, shy, quiet

M	L		#
☐	☐	Sociable, enjoys company of others	9
☐	☐	Patient, steady, tolerant	
☐	☐	Self-reliant, independent	
☐	☐	Soft-spoken, mild, reserved	
☐	☐	Adventurous, willing to take chances	10
☐	☐	Receptive, open to suggestions	
☐	☐	Cordial, warm, friendly	
☐	☐	Moderate, avoids extremes	
☐	☐	Talkative, chatty	11
☐	☐	Controlled, restrained	
☐	☐	Conventional, doing it the usual way, customary	
☐	☐	Decisive, certain, firm in making a decision	
☐	☐	Polished, smooth talker	12
☐	☐	Daring, risk-taker	
☐	☐	Diplomatic, tactful to people	
☐	☐	Satisfied, content, pleased	

M	L		#
☐	☐	Aggressive, challenger, takes action	13
☐	☐	Life of the party, outgoing, entertaining	
☐	☐	Easy mark, easily taken advantage of	
☐	☐	Fearful, afraid	
☐	☐	Cautious, wary, careful	14
☐	☐	Determined, decided, unwavering, stands firm	
☐	☐	Convincing, assuring	
☐	☐	Good-natured, pleasant	
☐	☐	Willing, go along with	15
☐	☐	Eager, anxious	
☐	☐	Agreeable, consenting	
☐	☐	High-spirited, lively, enthusiastic	
☐	☐	Confident, believes in self, assured	16
☐	☐	Sympathetic, compassionate, understanding	
☐	☐	Tolerant	
☐	☐	Assertive, aggressive	

M	L	17	M	L	21
☐	☐	Well-disciplined, self-controlled	☐	☐	Trusting, faith in others
☐	☐	Generous, willing to share	☐	☐	Contented, satisfied
☐	☐	Animated, uses gestures for expression	☐	☐	Positive, admitting no doubt
☐	☐	Persistent, unrelenting, refuses to quit	☐	☐	Peaceful, tranquil
		18			**22**
☐	☐	Admirable, deserving of praise	☐	☐	Good mixer, likes being with others
☐	☐	Kind, willing to give or help	☐	☐	Cultured, educated, knowledgeable
☐	☐	Resigned, gives in	☐	☐	Vigorous, energetic
☐	☐	Force of character, powerful	☐	☐	Lenient, not overly strict, tolerant of others' actions
		19			**23**
☐	☐	Respectful, shows respect	☐	☐	Companionable, easy to be with
☐	☐	Pioneering, exploring, enterprising	☐	☐	Accurate, correct
☐	☐	Optimistic, positive view	☐	☐	Outspoken, speaks freely and boldly
☐	☐	Accommodating, willing to please, ready to help	☐	☐	Restrained, reserved, controlled
		20			**24**
☐	☐	Argumentative, confronting	☐	☐	Restless, unable to rest or relax
☐	☐	Adaptable, flexible	☐	☐	Neighborly, friendly
☐	☐	Nonchalant, casually indifferent	☐	☐	Popular, liked by many or most people
☐	☐	Light-hearted, carefree	☐	☐	Orderly, neat, organized

PERSONAL INTERESTS AND VALUES SURVEY

Personal values are those interests, goals, and preferences that guide our lives and careers. This instrument is designed to help you determine which particular area of preference is most important to you.

Please read the directions completely and print your data.

There are twelve categories for response, each with six items for you to consider. This is not a timed response, but please take only the time you need to complete this form.

Directions

Mark your personal preference in each of the twelve areas listed below. Rank each of the six statements by indicating your choices in numerical order. Your first choice is 1, your second choice is 2, your third choice is 3, and so on. Each number must be used once in each of the twelve groups, and each blank must be completed.

Example:

PERSONAL INTERESTS

__3__ Independence
__6__ Joining a group with traditions
__5__ Appreciation of the beauty of nature
__2__ Money
__4__ Service to others
__1__ Knowledge

NAME ____________________ ADDRESS ____________________

PHONE (w) ______________ (h) ______________ MALE _____ FEMALE _____

1 My favorite subjects to study:
_____ Math/Science
_____ Political Science
_____ Theology
_____ Fine Arts
_____ Financial Planning
_____ Social Studies

2 My personal interests are:
_____ Independence
_____ Joining a group with traditions
_____ Appreciation of the beauty of nature
_____ Financial security
_____ Service to others
_____ Knowledge

3 Leisure activities that I enjoy:
_____ Volunteer work
_____ Studying new things
_____ Sports
_____ Investing or spending money
_____ Going to museums
_____ Thinking about life

4 Personal motivators for me are:
_____ Being a leader
_____ Continuing education
_____ Being a good citizen
_____ Helping others
_____ Increasing my net worth
_____ Arts/Crafts

5 My career goals:
_____ Artist
_____ Researcher
_____ Business owner
_____ Manager
_____ Historian
_____ Social reformer

6 My desire for improvement may include:
_____ Spiritual growth
_____ Helping others
_____ Leadership roles
_____ Security for retirement
_____ Additional education
_____ Beautification of personal surroundings

7 If I were given $500,000 I would:

_____ Purchase an art collection
_____ Start my own business
_____ Give some to charity
_____ Save some/Invest some
_____ Take courses to gain knowledge
_____ Donate to church fund

8 I think our tax money should be spent on:

_____ Help for the homeless
_____ Military/Defense
_____ Education
_____ Funding of the arts
_____ Reducing the federal deficit
_____ Drug control

9 People I admire as role models:

_____ Mother Teresa
_____ General George Patton
_____ John D. Rockefeller
_____ Michelangelo
_____ Albert Einstein
_____ Rev. Billy Graham

10 The way I would like to contribute to society:

_____ Helping the sick and disadvantaged
_____ Being a business person
_____ Being a team player
_____ Protecting the environment
_____ Being an inventor
_____ Initiator of community activities

11 My personal goals:

_____ Reformer
_____ Elected official
_____ Economic freedom
_____ Discovering new technology
_____ Artistic expression
_____ Personal growth

12 My outside interests:

_____ Teaching
_____ Acting
_____ Community projects
_____ Part-time business
_____ Politics
_____ Church activities